# THE HOLY SPIRIT

My Indispensable Friend

EMMANUEL ACHEAMPONG KUDJOE

Copyright © 2019 Emmanuel Acheampong Kudjoe.

All rights reserved. No part of this book may be used or reproduced by any means, graphic, electronic, or mechanical, including photocopying, recording, taping or by any information storage retrieval system without the written permission of the author except in the case of brief quotations embodied in critical articles and reviews.

This book is a work of non-fiction. Unless otherwise noted, the author and the publisher make no explicit guarantees as to the accuracy of the information contained in this book and in some cases, names of people and places have been altered to protect their privacy.

WestBow Press books may be ordered through booksellers or by contacting:

WestBow Press
A Division of Thomas Nelson & Zondervan
1663 Liberty Drive
Bloomington, IN 47403
www.westbowpress.com
1 (866) 928-1240

Because of the dynamic nature of the Internet, any web addresses or links contained in this book may have changed since publication and may no longer be valid. The views expressed in this work are solely those of the author and do not necessarily reflect the views of the publisher, and the publisher hereby disclaims any responsibility for them.

Any people depicted in stock imagery provided by Getty Images are models, and such images are being used for illustrative purposes only. Certain stock imagery © Getty Images.

Cover Design: Gloria Plange, Worcester, Massachusetts

Author's Photograph: AfricaBa Multimedia, Worcester, Massachusetts

ISBN: 978-1-9736-6586-1 (sc)
ISBN: 978-1-9736-6585-4 (hc)
ISBN: 978-1-9736-6587-8 (e)

Library of Congress Control Number: 2019907602

Print information available on the last page.

WestBow Press rev. date: 07/02/2019

Scripture quotations marked (NIV) are taken from the Holy Bible, New International Version®, NIV®. Copyright © 1973, 1978, 1984, 2011 by Biblica, Inc.™ Used by permission of Zondervan. All rights reserved worldwide. www.zondervan.com The "NIV" and "New International Version" are trademarks registered in the United States Patent and Trademark Office by Biblica, Inc.™

Scripture taken from the King James Version of the Bible.

Scripture quotations taken from the New American Standard Bible® (NASB), Copyright © 1960, 1962, 1963, 1968, 1971, 1972, 1973, 1975, 1977, 1995 by The Lockman Foundation Used by permission. www.Lockman.org

The Holy Bible, Berean Study Bible, BSB Copyright ©2016, 2018 by Bible Hub Used by Permission. All Rights Reserved Worldwide.

Scripture quotations marked (NLT) are taken from the Holy Bible, New Living Translation, copyright ©1996, 2004, 2015 by Tyndale House Foundation. Used by permission of Tyndale House Publishers, Inc., Carol Stream, Illinois 60188. All rights reserved.

Scripture quotations are from the ESV® Bible (The Holy Bible, English Standard Version®), copyright © 2001 by Crossway, a publishing ministry of Good News Publishers. Used by permission. All rights reserved.

Scripture quotations marked (AMP) are taken from the Amplified Bible, Copyright © 1954, 1958, 1962, 1964, 1965, 1987 by The Lockman Foundation. Used by permission.

Scripture taken from the New King James Version®. Copyright © 1982 by Thomas Nelson. Used by permission. All rights reserved.

Scripture quotations marked (CEV) are from the Contemporary English Version Copyright © 1991, 1992, 1995 by American Bible Society, Used by Permission.

Scripture quotations marked HCSB are taken from the Holman Christian Standard Bible®, Used by Permission HCSB ©1999,2000,2002,2003,2009 Holman Bible Publishers. Holman Christian Standard Bible®, Holman CSB®, and HCSB® are federally registered trademarks of Holman Bible Publishers.

# CONTENTS

**Part I   Initial Encounters**

CHAPTER 1   My Initial Encounter with the Holy Spirit . . . . . . . 1
CHAPTER 2   How the Universe Encountered Him . . . . . . . . . . 21

**Part II   The Holy Spirit: Who Is He—
and Why Is He Indispensable?**

CHAPTER 3   Indispensable Characteristics I . . . . . . . . . . . . . . . 33
CHAPTER 4   Indispensable Characteristics II. . . . . . . . . . . . . . . 51
CHAPTER 5   Indispensable in Old Testament Ministry . . . . . . 83
CHAPTER 6   Indispensable in the Life and Ministry of Jesus . 97
CHAPTER 7   Indispensable in the First-Century Church . . . . 109
CHAPTER 8   Indispensable Giver of Power . . . . . . . . . . . . . . . . 133
CHAPTER 9   Indispensable for End-Time Ministry . . . . . . . . . 171

**Part III   How You Can Experience the Holy
Spirit as Your Indispensable Friend**

CHAPTER 10  You Can Enjoy His Indispensable Fullness . . . . 209
CHAPTER 11  Be Led by the Indispensable Spirit. . . . . . . . . . . . 223
CHAPTER 12  Yield! Yield! Yield! . . . . . . . . . . . . . . . . . . . . . . . . . . 235

# FOREWORD

"The Holy Spirit: My Indispensable Friend" can be summed up in one word…AWESOME!

We are living in a day that our relationship with the Holy Spirit must be as real as any of our earthly relationships. The time is upon us that we must be familiar with the Holy Spirit's leading and His voice, that when He directs us to go here or there, we go.

I recently heard a story regarding Druid Priests, that every year would put their boat in the water without oars or a rudder. They would trust the Holy Spirit to take them where they were supposed to be. When they arrived at one island, there was a man standing at the shoreline who told them they had been waiting for them. The same is true for today, there are people and places that are waiting for us to come and release the power of the Holy Spirit residing inside of us.

I believe that this next great move of God will be a release of the power and the glory of the Holy Spirit. As I read through "The Holy Spirit: My Indispensable Friend", I began to think about Benny Hinn's book "Good Morning Holy Spirit". But, I believe this book is for today and I believe the book will bring a fresh hunger and thirst to know the Holy Spirit in a personal and intimate way! I really believe this book is going to be a best seller!! I have no doubt in my mind that God has inspired the writing of this book to teach believers how to build a personal relationship with the Holy Spirit not only as guide, helper, teacher and revealer of divine agenda, but as our Friend that is closer to us than a brother.

Rev. Deborah J. Smith
Life Christian University, Tampa, Florida
Main Campus Director/Director of Online Learning

# PREFACE

On May 6, 2013, when I was done preaching a sermon titled "The Expediency of the Holy Spirit," a guest came to me and introduced himself as a pastor from New York. He told how much he was blessed by my message. "As you spoke" he said, "I could see you had more in you than time would allow. How about preaching it as a series or better still developing it into a book?" He was right; I did have much more in me than I could deliver in forty minutes. After much prayer and study, I became convinced that the best way to share what was burning in my heart was to put it into writing.

This book discusses the indispensable role the Holy Spirit plays in the life of the Christian as well as in the Church. The Holy Spirit is the Christian's inexhaustible source of power and grace for Christlike living and fruitful ministry. The Holy Spirit makes it possible for us to be born again, and He stands ready to lead us every step of the way through life's journey. He is our constant help, guide, and teacher. You will discover, through the many stories I share in this book, that I have found Him to be my indispensable friend—and He can be yours as well!

Please join me as we explore the indispensability of the Holy Spirit in all of God's dealings with humankind—from creation and all the people God used mightily in the Old Testament, in the life and ministry of Jesus, to the first-century Church. You will discover God's ordained roles of the Holy Spirit in the contemporary church, and more importantly, you will learn how you can tap into the fullness and power of the Holy Spirit and live every minute of your life in the refreshing presence of Almighty God. The Holy Spirit is waiting to lead you into the amazing life in the supernatural. Are you ready for this exciting journey? I know you are. Let's get started!

# ACKNOWLEDGMENTS

I couldn't have written this book without the help of the many wonderful people God placed in my path. My first thanks go to my Bible College professor, Rev. Deborah J. Smith, Director of Main Campus and Online Learning, Life Christian University, for taking time off her busy schedule to read through my manuscript and for writing the preface to this book. Rev. Deb, I can't thank you enough for believing in me and the grace of God on my life and ministry. Your powerful words in the preface will, no doubt, whet the appetite of readers to crave a closer walk with the Holy Spirit.

In writing this book, I put together a small team of young adults to critique the work and provide objective feedback from the perspective of a reader. Comprising Oti Achamfour, George Odartey Lamptey, and Vivian Boateng, my "A Team" spent many hours questioning and challenging me to bring the best out of me. A Team, I am eternally thankful to God for bringing you into my life. I am grateful to you for your sacrifice, skills, and commitment to excellence.

To John Jones, my accountability brother in Atlanta, Georgia, I say thanks for critiquing my initial manuscript and encouraging me "not to be too 'preachy' but tell your story." I am also indebted to Elder George Anim and Mrs. Abena Anim, of PIWC, Worcester, who graciously read the very first manuscript in 2014 and helped shape the trajectory of the book. Yaw Safo-Poku, for urging me to share more stories of my personal experiences with the Holy Spirit, I thank you.

Gloria Plange, I owe you tons of thanks for the many hours you devoted to designing the cover of the book. Mama G, you are definitely the best! I thank Rev. Gerald Plange, General Overseer of Upper Room Family International Church (URFIC), Mrs. Irene Plange, First Lady of URFIC, Worcester, and all the ministers of URFIC for your encouragement and prayer support, and for giving me the platform to test the principles described in this book.

Bob Flaherty, my big brother and friend, thanks for your helpful suggestions. To the members of URFIC, Leominster, my flock, I say you are Godsent, and I love you all. I thank my wife and children for their loving and prayerful support. Finally, I thank the staff of WestBow Press for their professionalism throughout this journey.

I dedicate this book to you if you are:

- thirsting for the refreshing water of the Holy Spirit;
- craving to be used of God to your fullest potential; and
- yearning to walk in the fullness and power of the Holy Spirit.

# PART I
## Initial Encounters

# Chapter 1

## My Initial Encounter with the Holy Spirit

*Ministry is much easier and more exciting
if it is done with the Holy Spirit.*

LIKE COLD WATER TO a weary soul is good news from a distant land. (Proverbs 25:25 NIV) We heard about it and welcomed it from afar. The long-awaited day had finally come. It was almost as if the hand of time had just pulled it out of the laps of eternity, creating a palpable ecstasy in the otherwise quiet town.

The Anglican bishop in charge of the southern region was visiting the small diocese in my town. The anticipation and euphoria in the air were so thick that one could cut through them with a knife. It was only morning, but the sun was already out of its habitation and was ready to run its course. The day seemed sacred and felt like a whiff of holiness had escaped from heaven's chimney into our town.

Drivers were honking their horns, pedestrians were crossing the streets from all angles, and children were weaving through the crowd to catch a glimpse of what was yet to unfold. The scene was like a replay of the triumphant entry into Jerusalem save the greenery and the asphalt road that were the pride and joy of my town. The joy of anticipation kept brewing in my restless heart. My imagination was invaded with a plethora of images about a bishop I had never seen before. In my mind's eye, I envisioned a tall, handsome man in a purple cassock and long miter that pointed to the sky. I thought peradventure he would also bear some resemblance to my beloved uncle, who had gone to be with the Lord a couple of months earlier.

When the bishop finally arrived, he looked nothing like the trickery my imagination had created. His captivating demeanor, however, compensated for his petite frame. On setting my eyes on him, I almost jumped out of my dark skin for joy. I stretched out my head so I could snatch my portion of blessing from him. With shouts of joy and cheers rising to a crescendo from the townsfolk, the bishop and his entourage were ushered into the sanctuary. As they entered, the bishop solemnly laid his hands on all the children within his reach and blessed them. Guess what. I was one of them!

Then came the moment we had been waiting for: the sermon. The bishop first spoke in English and then translated his message to the native Fante dialect. For some strange reason I couldn't explain, his words made a memorable impression on me. Using John 16:7, the bishop preached on the expediency of the Holy Spirit.

> Nevertheless, I tell you the truth; *it is expedient for you* that I go away: for if I go not away, *the Comforter* will not come unto you; but if I depart, *I will send Him unto you.* (John 16:7 KJV, emphasis mine)

It was the first time I had heard of the Holy Spirit. At age nine, I could not understand much of the bishop's sermon, but somehow, I got the sense that the Holy Spirit is a must-have in the life of every Christian. That theme stuck with me. Though more than four decades have passed since I heard the bishop's sermon, I can still remember the solemn atmosphere that filled the little church building as he spoke. "I tell you the truth; it is expedient for you that I go away: for if I go not away, the Comforter will not come unto you" (John 16:7 KJV). From time to time, the verse would ring in my mind, and I would hear the Anglican bishop's deep, calm voice bellow.

Raised in a strict Presbyterian home, I was a well-mannered boy. My calm temperament, excellent academic performance, and adherence to school rules made me every teacher's darling boy. At age ten, I was presented a special award for being the best-behaved student of my school. For my prize, I was given a small book of prayers. I memorized most of its prayers and recited them during our family's morning devotions and sometimes at school. While people were impressed with my prayers, I felt a sense of emptiness. Deep within me, I desired to know God, but for some strange reason, He seemed far away from me.

About a year after the bishop's visit, one of my classmates, Patrick, came to school with a leap in his step and a glow in his eyes. When we inquired what was going on, he exclaimed, "I'm born again! I'm born again! Praise God! I'm born again!" Knowing him as a trickster, we received his statements with a grain of salt. However, after observing him for several weeks, we noticed that he no longer used bad words or laughed when other boys said coarse jokes, and he no longer stole other students' pencils and erasers. We all concluded that Patrick's spiritual experience was real. He became more focused on his studies than before, and his efforts were rewarded with significant improvement in his academic performance.

During breaks, Patrick would take his Gideon's New Testament and read. Whenever, he volunteered to pray at our school assembly, his prayers sounded different from the prayers I had memorized from my prayer book. He prayed as if he actually knew God. There was no denying that Patrick had experienced a drastic transformation in his life. He also seemed to have developed a new set of vocabulary and spoke with new confidence. I was amazed at Patrick's newfound boldness, his accelerated spiritual growth, and his maturity.

In conversation one day, Patrick told me the source of his new life was the Holy Spirit. He said he had been baptized in the Holy Spirit and prayed in an unknown language. I couldn't make head or tail of what he said except that it seemed very strange to me. Though I did not know what to make of these things, I was certain about one thing: Patrick had had a real life-transforming experience, and he attributed it to the Holy Spirit. Patrick's changed life reminded me of the bishop's message.

Three years after the bishop's visit, I gained admission to a boarding high school. During the first week, a senior boy invited me to the school's Christian fellowship. The meeting flowed nicely with simple-to-follow choruses and songs of praise. After a short time of prayer, the president of the group stepped to the lectern and presented a short message. He made four main points.

1. God loves us (John 3:16).
2. All of us have turned our backs on God. We have lost our way, and we are deserving of God's punishment (Rom. 3:23; Isa. 53:6).
3. God has provided a way back to Himself through the death of His Son, Jesus, on the cross (Rom. 5:8).
4. Those who repent of their sins and invite Jesus Christ into their lives as their personal Savior and Lord shall be forgiven and saved (Rom. 10:9–10; Acts 4:12).

As he spoke, I recalled the bishop's sermon and wondered whether this was the same born-again experience Patrick had spoken about. If this was Patrick's experience, then I wanted it. When the preacher asked who wanted to receive Jesus Christ as their personal Lord and Savior to come forward, I and many other students stepped forward and prayed at the altar.

Surprisingly, I felt a new peace in my heart after inviting Jesus into my life. Prior to this, I lived in constant fear of death because three of my four uncles had died within five years. I wondered why my uncles had died in rapid succession during the prime of their lives and was afraid my remaining uncle might also die young. Growing up, my eldest uncle was my role model. As a young boy, I was enthralled with him and wanted to be like him. He was a good man and treated me like his own. Tragically, he went to be with the Lord in a fatal car crash a few months before the bishop's scheduled visit. His death sent me down a spiral of uncertainty, anxiety, and fear. Nights were restless, and sound sleep was a rarity.

Surrendering my life to Jesus Christ broke the back of that oppressive fear that had haunted me for five years! Not only did God set me free from the bondage of sin, but He also delivered me from the depressive fear of premature death. And He gave me His peace that surpasses all understanding. In place of despair, the Lord filled my heart with hope of eternal life.

After my born-again experience, the leaders of the fellowship taught me to read my Bible and pray every morning before we began our normal school chores. Our slogan was "NBNB," meaning "No Bible, no breakfast." I learned to have a personal quiet time with the Lord at dawn, during which I read a short passage of scripture and prayed. Though my quiet time took only about fifteen minutes, it provided me with the spiritual strength I needed to live a godly life in the midst of so much godlessness around me.

A few weeks after my new-birth experience, my closest friend, Sammy, who had been born again a couple of years earlier, told me about his experience with the Holy Spirit. His boldness, joy, and obvious sweet intimacy with God left my mind in inquisition. Clearly, his profound words traced their way to my heart. The president of the fellowship, who happened to be in my dormitory, also shared with me many stories about how the Holy Spirit spoke to him and guided him every day. Some of the things he told me seemed strange to me. For example, he told me that sometimes he would wake up speaking in tongues. He also told me the Holy Spirit often revealed future events to him in a vision and dreams before those events happened. These testimonies created in me a spiritual thirst for a deeper experience with the Holy Spirit. I began to long for a deeper personal relationship with the Holy Spirit. Any time I thought about the Holy Spirit, I would hear the bishop's deep voice ring Jesus's words:

> Nevertheless, I tell you the truth; *it is expedient for you* that I go away: for if I go not away, *the Comforter* will not come unto you; but if I depart, *I will send Him unto you.* (John 16:7 KJV, emphasis mine)

As I reflected on this verse, I realized that while this promise was in the future for the disciples, it was here and now for me. Jesus has already gone to the Father and has already sent the Holy Spirit. It was now up to me to find out from the Word of God how I could tap into the benefits the Comforter provided. As I sought the face of God concerning this matter, the Holy Spirit took me through a series of events, which culminated in a life-transforming encounter with Him.

## My Pendulum Experience

The years following my conversion could best be described as a pendulum experience. I was exposed to two apparent contradictory teachings on the Holy Spirit. I will describe the first school of thought as the "one-step experience" and the second one as the "two-step experience."

## The One-Step Experience School of Thought

The one-step experience proponents taught that conversion and baptism in the Holy Spirit took place simultaneously when you received Jesus as your personal Savior. They also taught that since all born-again Christians have the Holy Spirit living in them, there was no need for a second experience called baptism in the Holy Spirit. The main supporting scriptures they used were 1

*The Holy Spirit*

Corinthians 12:12–13 and Romans 8:14–16. In Corinthians 12:12–13, the Bible says:

> The body is a unit, though it is made up of many parts; and though all its parts are many, they form one body. So it is with Christ. For we were all baptized by one Spirit into one body—whether Jews or Greeks, slave or free—and we were all given the one Spirit to drink. (1 Cor. 12:12–13 NIV)

The proponents of this school of thought interpreted this passage of scripture to mean that at conversion all Christians were baptized by the Holy Spirit into one body i.e. Christ. They also supported their position with Romans 8:14–16, which says:

> Those who are led by the Spirit of God are sons of God. For you did not receive a spirit that makes you a slave again to fear, but you received the Spirit of sonship. And by him we cry, "Abba," "Father." The Spirit himself testifies with our spirit that we are God's children (Rom. 8:14–16 NIV).

We were taught that this scripture means that we received the Holy Spirit at conversion and that made us children of God. The one-step experience school of thought also taught that subsequent to conversion, all you have to do is to continuously ask the Holy Spirit to fill you for victorious living and effective ministry. The supporting scripture is "Do not get drunk on wine, which leads to debauchery. Instead, be filled with the Spirit (Eph. 5:18 NIV). My brothers who held this position asserted that there was no external or outward evidence of being filled with the Holy Spirit. They also taught that speaking in tongues was one of the gifts of the Holy Spirit and it was not meant for all Christians. It was the prerogative of the Holy Spirit to determine which gift to give to each Christian, they claimed. 1 Corinthians 12:4–11 was used to support this position.

> There are different kinds of gifts, but the same Spirit. There are different kinds of service, but the same Lord. There are different kinds of working, but the same God works all of them in all men. Now to each one the manifestation of the Spirit is given for the common good. To one there is given through the Spirit the message of wisdom, to another the message of knowledge by means of the same Spirit, to another faith by the same Spirit, to another gifts of healing by that one Spirit, 1to another miraculous powers, to another prophecy, to another distinguishing between spirits, to another speaking in different kinds of tongues, and to still another the interpretation of tongues. All these are the work of one and the same Spirit, and he gives them to each one, just as he determines (1 Cor. 12:4–11 NIV).

## The Two-Step Experience School of Thought

The two-step Holy Spirit experience school of thought, on the other hand, asserted that God has made available to every born-again Christian a second experience subsequent to conversion called baptism in the Holy Spirit. According to this school of thought, the initial outward evidence that one has received the baptism in the Holy Spirit is *glossolalia*, the phenomenon of speaking in a language other than one's native language as enabled by the Holy Spirit. The two-step experience school of thought made a distinction between speaking in tongues as evidence of the baptism in the Holy Spirit, which is available to all believers, and speaking in diverse kinds of tongues as one of the gifts the Holy Spirit gives to some Christians.

*The Holy Spirit*

My primary allegiance was to the one-step experience school of thought, mainly because that was the official position of the Christian fellowship I was a staunch member and eventually a leader of. At our camp meetings, the leaders of the one-step experience ridiculed our brothers and sisters who believed in the two-step experience. Adherents of the two-step experience position were portrayed as fanatical blockheads who allowed their emotions to get the better of them. Ironically, there were many brothers and sisters in our group, who happened to have had the two-step experience but who kept their experience under wraps for fear of being labeled "fanatics."

About two months after I became president of my school's Christian fellowship, an alumnus of my school came to visit us. He told us about his dramatic encounter with the Lord. His testimony was very powerful because we all knew him as one of those students who had a penchant for getting into trouble and not caring very much about his appearance. Here he was speaking politely, neatly dressed, and studying engineering in the most prestigious technology university in the country. He ascribed the change in his life to Jesus, and we praised God for that. However, when he began to share with us about his two-step experience, I vehemently opposed him and interrupted him several times, thus preventing him from sharing his message in a coherent manner with the group. At the time, I thought I was doing my duty because at our leadership training sessions, we were taught to oppose such "heresies."

Meanwhile, I had an insatiable thirst for more of God. My friends in the two-step experience school of thought seemed to have a depth of power, level of practical faith, intimacy with God, and infectious joy that I lacked. At prayer meetings, they could pray for hours without getting tired. In contrast, I usually ran out of words in minutes, and my mind would wander outside the room.

While reading Morris Cerullo's *Proof Producers*, I learned that God wanted to use ordinary people to accomplish His supernatural purpose. Quoting Jesus's words in John 14:12, "Very truly I tell you, whoever believes in me will do the works I have been doing, and they will do even greater things than these, because I am going to the Father" (NIV), Dr. Cerullo explained that God wanted His people to go beyond receiving His blessing to the point where they could demonstrate the power of God. In other words, God was looking for people through whom He would produce proof of His power, grace, and love just as He did through Jesus. The message in the book fired me up to seek God for the baptism in the Holy Spirit. Unfortunately, while my heart wanted it, my mind continued to oppose it. Being of two minds, I received nothing, just as the Bible says: "That person should not expect to receive anything from the Lord. Such a person is double-minded and unstable in all they do" (James 1:7–8 NIV).

As time passed, I felt increasingly inadequate. One night, in a discussion with my friend Sammy, he made a statement that hit me like a thunderbolt: "It's God's will for every Christian to speak in tongues."

I quickly responded, "What? Isn't speaking in tongues one of the gifts of the Holy Spirit, and doesn't the Holy Spirit give His gifts as He chooses?"

With a look of compassion and in his usual calm demeanor, Sammy explained that when Paul wrote to the Corinthian believers "I wish *all* of you spoke in tongues" (1 Cor. 14:5 NASB, emphasis mine), he was expressing God's desire for every believer. "Anyone who speaks in a tongue edifies himself," Sammy told me, quoting 1 Corinthians 14:4 (Berean Study Bible). He asked me directly, "Wouldn't you want the Holy Spirit to help you edify yourself every time you pray?"

His words hit me like a rock, but again, the stronghold of the one-step experience school of thought in me protested. My guard was always up, and my heart was closed to the blessing of the Holy Spirit. The result was the restlessness in my spirit continued. Though I experienced "sprinkles" from the fountain of the Holy Spirit, I knew God wanted me to tap into the fullness of the Holy Spirit. Reluctantly, I began to ask God to forgive me for my hardness of heart and to show me what to do.

## Supernatural Encounter

My school had an "exchange-of-pulpits" arrangement with a neighboring school. Every other week, a student from my school's Christian fellowship would go and preach in the other school's fellowship while they also sent one of their students to preach in our fellowship. One day, a brother from the sister school came and told us they were expecting one of us to preach in their meeting. I had just been elected president of my school's fellowship and was not aware of the schedule. Since it was impossible to ask anyone to go on such short notice, I had no option but to go myself. The problem, however, was that I was completely at sea. I was unprepared. I had no message to share. No theme to develop. No Bible text. Absolutely nothing! All the messages I had previously prepared and preached had evaporated. I felt helpless as my mind went completely blank. Every Bible verse I had memorized raced out of my mind.

As I walked with the brother to their school, he began to pray in tongues. I tried to pray, but I couldn't find the words to say. Momentarily, I felt the Holy Spirit was helping this brother gain special access to God—nothing like the one I had. At that moment, I wished I could switch to this supernatural means of prayer and possibly receive a message from God. Out of desperation, I just whispered under my breath, "Holy Spirit, please help me. Please give me a message. Holy Spirit, please speak through me."

We had hardly settled into our seats when the president of the sister school's fellowship introduced me to preach. With my feet quaking and mouth trembling, I stepped forward and offered one of the sincerest prayers I have ever prayed in my life: "Lord God Almighty, you know I have no message, but I thank you that you promised to send your Holy Spirit to help me. So, Holy Spirit, please give me a word. Please speak through me."

While I was praying, I began to feel the presence of the Holy Spirit in a tangible way. I suddenly became bold and relaxed. All the heaviness left me, and I began to speak as the Holy Spirit gave me the words. The Holy Spirit spoke to me through my right ear, and I simply repeated what He said to me. Sentence by sentence, I repeated what He told me. When He was done, He said, "Amen," and I repeated it. I then prayed, "Thank you, Holy Spirit, my Helper, for speaking through me. I give you all the glory in Jesus's name." The message was short and powerful. It was the Word of God in the true sense of the phrase because I spoke as the Holy Spirit dictated the words to me. It was an amazing experience!

I took away three things from that supernatural experience. First, I learned that the Holy Spirit is my ever-present helper. Second, ministry is much easier and more exciting if it is done with the Holy Spirit. Third, the Holy Spirit is waiting on us to call on Him to partner with Him to get God's work on earth done, and when we do, He will lead us, teach us, empower us, and work through us.

> **Remember**
>
> *Ministry is much easier and more exciting if it is done with the Holy Spirit.*

I was sixteen years old, and this experience marked the beginning of my intimate journey with the Holy Spirit. Shortly after this, I ran into a revival service of a well-known preacher I admired. When I got there, he had just finished his sermon and was making the altar call for those who wished to receive Jesus as their Lord and personal Savior. After that, he called for those who were thirsty for the fullness of the Holy Spirit to come forward. For the first time, I found this preacher's approach nonthreatening and even welcoming.

There was a sweet presence of the Holy Spirit in the auditorium. The preacher explained, "If you are born again, the Holy Spirit already lives in you." I found that comforting. He also explained that, according to John 7:39, the Holy Spirit in you wants to be

*The Holy Spirit*

"released" so He can flow out like streams of living water to make you much more effective. The only condition for receiving this overflow of the Holy Spirit is to be thirsty.

> On the last and greatest day of the festival, Jesus stood and said in a loud voice, "Let anyone who is thirsty come to me and drink. Whoever believes in me, as scripture has said, rivers of living water will flow from within them." By this he meant the Spirit, whom those who believed in him were later to receive. Up to that time the Spirit had not been given, since Jesus had not yet been glorified. (John 7:37–39 NIV)

Immediately, the scales fell off my eyes. With my heart receptive and my mind ready, I went forward to have the man of God lay his hands on me. I was so full of faith that the moment he reached out to touch me, I felt a powerful release of joy flowing from inside of me up through my throat and then out of my mouth. Suddenly, I found myself praising God out loud in other tongues.

The joy I felt was boundless. My hands were up in the air, praising God. I don't know how long I remained at the altar, but I knew I was right in the presence of Almighty God, and it felt good! It felt like I was walking on thin air. My burdens were rolled away. As I walked home that night, I kept praising God in tongues in the street, caring very little what anybody thought about me. Something supernatural had happened to me, and I had to praise God for it!

The days following this experience were wonderful. I seized all the free time I had to pray. Prayer was no longer a chore but a joy. I immersed myself in long hours of prayer and worship. The scriptures came alive in a fresh way whenever I studied the Bible. The Holy Spirit literally became my teacher. He gave me a deeper understanding of and insight into God's Word. Sometimes, when I read the Bible, the Holy Spirit would create the setting of the passage right before my eyes. It was almost like He transported me to the historical context of the passage I was reading and explained the meaning of the passage to me. This experience with the Holy Spirit enabled me to teach the Bible with authority, clarity, and freshness.

Another change that took place after my two-step Holy Spirit experience was that it opened to me the floodgates of the gifts of the Holy Spirit. In addition to speaking in tongues, the Holy Spirit gave me the gifts of prophecy and interpretation of tongues. Sometimes, the Holy Spirit would reveal things about certain people to me, and when I said it, it was spot-on. The Bible calls this gift the "Word of Knowledge." To ensure the effective use of the gift of Word of Knowledge, the Holy Spirit also gave me the gift of Word of Wisdom, which enables me to speak forth a revelation at the right time and in the appropriate fashion. On different occasions, the Holy Spirit has enabled me to operate in the gift of healing and discerning of spirits, according to the need at hand. Like everything God gives, I had to learn the proper use of the gifts of the Holy Spirit.

On the eve of a Gospel crusade, a certain woman invited us to go and pray for her sick mom. The sick woman had been bedfast for days. While we were praying, the Holy Spirit showed me, in a vision, that the woman was bound with concentric iron bars. I shared with the group what the Holy Spirit had shown me. We intensified our prayer and commanded the satanic bondage to be broken. About ten minutes later, I had a second vision in which I saw a big pair of hands cutting the iron bars with a chainsaw. As soon as I shared the second vision, we all began thanking God for the answered prayer. The woman sat up on the bed unaided and began praising God with us. She was completely healed and got out of bed all by herself; she testified to her healing during our Gospel crusade.

The Holy Spirit has been my closest, most intimate friend and helper. He speaks to me anywhere, including in the shower and when I'm shaving, preparing meals, or doing dishes. The Holy

Spirit speaks to me in a gentle but authoritative manner. We have developed such intimacy that I have no doubt when He speaks to me. Most times, His voice comes as a gentle impression or a whisper in my ear. When I pause and pay attention, He goes ahead to tell me what's in God's heart. What really amazes me is that sometimes the Holy Spirit tells me even little things before they happen. For example, during my private time of prayer and Bible study, the Holy Spirit usually reveals to me events that would happen in course of the day. This revelation really serves me well because it allows me to pray and prepare for those events, especially if they are unpleasant.

I have seen many Christians relate to the Holy Spirit as their indispensable friend. My exposure to the lives of my spirit-filled friends has taught me that ordinary believers can experience unbroken intimate friendship with the Holy Spirit. Through the study of the Bible and my own experience, I am convinced that God wants all Christians to be led by the Holy Spirit. God wants us to learn to hear the voice of the Holy Spirit and to respond to it. He also wants us to be constantly and consistently filled with His Spirit, produce spiritual fruit, and exercise spiritual power on His behalf through the gifts of the Spirit and by living lives worthy of our resurrected Christ. This is the normal Christian life.

**Reflection on my Pendulum Experience**

I took a couple of things away from my pendulum experience. First, it seems to me that my one-step experience friends were trying to explain something they had not experienced, while my two-step experience friends had an experience they could not explain satisfactorily. In His infinite wisdom, God sometimes

> **Remember**
>
> *In His infinite wisdom, God sometimes gives us spiritual experiences before we get to understand what they really mean.*

gives us spiritual experiences before we get to understand what they really mean. Consider the new birth experience, for example. How many of us really understood what it means to be born again before we accepted the free gift of eternal life? Of course we did not try to understand everything about salvation before receiving it. We simply believed the message with our hearts, repented of our sin, prayed a simple prayer of faith, and our lives were changed. Then, as we studied or were taught the Word of God, we began to understand more and more about our salvation experience.

The same is true with the Holy Spirit. If we want to understand everything about the Holy Spirit, we will never experience the fullness of the Spirit. All we need to do is to open up to what God has plainly stated in His Word (concerning the Holy Spirit) in order to enjoy the full measure of what the Holy Spirit offers. God will not give us more light (understanding) until we humbly embrace and utilize the light He has already given us. Let me illustrate with the following example.

> **Remember**
>
> *God will not give us more light (understanding) until we humbly embrace and utilize the light He has already given us.*

When I was nineteen years old, I shared the Gospel with a sixteen-year-old girl named Matilda. She believed the message, repented of her sin, and asked Jesus to be the Lord and Savior of her life. I also shared with her how she could grow spiritually through daily Bible reading, prayer, fellowship, and sharing her faith. I started her off with a Gideon's New Testament and "Our Daily Bread" devotional. Three days later, I invited her to a home cell meeting. While, we were praying, I heard Matilda saying, "Lord, take all of me. Please take all of me." Suddenly she began to speak in tongues, praising God, and prophesying. Her experience reminded me of what happened at Cornelius house in Acts 10:44–48.

> While Peter was still speaking ... the Holy Spirit fell upon all those who were listening to the message. All the circumcised believers who came with Peter were amazed, because the gift of the Holy Spirit had been poured out on the Gentiles also. For they were hearing them speaking with tongues and exalting God. Then Peter answered, "Surely no one can refuse the water for these to be baptized who have received the Holy Spirit just as we did, can he?" And he ordered them to be baptized in the name of Jesus Christ. Then they asked him to stay on for a few days. (Acts 10:44–48 NASB)

Everything about this incident contradicted Jewish beliefs. Jews were not supposed to associate with Gentiles, let alone go to their homes, but Peter and his entourage did so in obedience to the direction of the Holy Spirit (Acts 10:28–29,19). Then while Peter was still sharing the Gospel with Cornelius and his household, the Holy Spirit fell upon all those who were listening to the message (Acts 10:44 NLT). The Jews who accompanied Peter were understandably amazed by this sovereign intervention because they did not expect Gentiles to partake in the blessings of God. I believe God poured the Holy Spirit on the Gentiles without any human involvement for at least two reasons: to bear witness to His Word and to fulfill His promise to pour out His Spirit upon *all flesh*—irrespective of nationality, culture, race, socioeconomic status, or educational background. The Holy Spirit is for everyone and anyone who will open up to Him.

> **Remember**
>
> *What the Holy Spirit does is sometimes unexplainable but it is undeniable because it is in your face.*

Like the Jewish believers who

accompanied Peter, I was pleasantly surprised by what the Lord did in Matilda's life. No human being had a hand in it. No one laid hands on her. The Holy Spirit fell upon her as she opened up to Him. For the next several days, I taught Matilda about the Holy Spirit and how she could effectively operate the gifts God had graciously given her. The point here is, God gave the experience first, and then the understanding followed. It is also important to point out that what the Holy Spirit does is sometimes unexplainable, but it is undeniable because it is in your face.

**Second Takeaway**

My second takeaway from my pendulum experience is that both schools of thought are partially right. I believe the one-step experience proponents are right in saying that we do receive the Holy Spirit at conversion. I do not know of any Christian group that teaches otherwise. Jesus said the Holy Spirit gives birth to our spiritual life (John 3:6). In Titus 3:5, the Bible says God saved us "through the washing of rebirth and renewal by the Holy Spirit" (NIV). This means our salvation was made possible through two powerful agencies: the Word of God, which washed us (Eph. 5:26; John 15:3), and the Holy Spirit who regenerated us.

I believe the two-step experience proponents are also right when they say that the Bible speaks of a second "receiving of the Holy Spirit," which is called baptism in the Holy Spirit. The Bible is replete with many examples of people who "received the Holy Spirit" after their new birth experience, including the disciples of Jesus (John 20:21–22; Acts 2:1–4), Paul (Acts 9:11–18), the believers in Samaria (Acts 8:14–17), and the disciples at Ephesus (Acts 19:1–7). With the exception of Cornelius and his family, who received the Holy Spirit while Peter was still speaking, throughout the recorded history of the first-century Church, people received the baptism in the Holy Spirit subsequent to their conversion. I will throw more light on this in chapter 8.

Another area of contention has to do with the terminologies

we used in discussing our experiences with the Holy Spirit. For example, do the following terminologies refer to one and the same experience: baptism in the Holy Spirit, filling with the Holy Spirit, infilling of the Holy Spirit, fullness of the Holy Spirit, and receiving the Holy Spirit? Again, I will discuss these issues in chapter 8.

**Chapter Takeaway**

My experience on both sides of the pendulum has made me exceptionally understanding and respectful of both positions. I have shared my experience in the hope that whatever your position is, you'll understand that God has a depth of powerful, untapped blessings and resources for getting His work on earth done. The fields are white, and the harvest is ready. Lost souls can only be won through the power of the Holy Spirit.

Think about this. If the disciples of Jesus, who were personally mentored by the Lord Himself, needed the Holy Spirit's empowerment to fulfill their divine calling, how much more do we need? My prayer for you is that the Lord will grant you an insatiable thirst for the fullness the Holy Spirit and a deeper craving to experience Him as your indispensable helper in life's journey.

# Chapter 2

## How the Universe Encountered Him

*The Spirit of God has made me; the
breath of the Almighty gives me life.*
—Job 33:4 (NIV)

A GREAT MYSTERY WAS ABOUT to unfold. The eternal, transcendent God had made a decision, a decision that defies human understanding. Elohim, the all-powerful Creator was on a mission, a mission to create a time-space realm where the timeless would relate to the time-bound. He had just stepped out of eternity into time without relinquishing His eternal qualities. The angelic hosts watched spellbound as the infinitely wise Creator spoke the heavens into existence and laid the foundations of the earth with His hands (Gen. 1:1; Heb. 1:10; Isa. 48:13).

Total darkness had covered the deep. The vast expanse of the universe was without form or shape. There was chaos everywhere. Suddenly, the Spirit of the LORD began to move over the face of the deep. Like a powerful bird jealously guarding its eggs, the Spirit hovered over the waters. There was absolute silence, save the incubation sound of the Holy Spirit. The angels continued to watch with rapt attention mixed with wonder.

Suddenly, without warning, God thundered, "Let there be light!" (Gen. 1:3a NIV). His voice, more powerful than the sound of many waters, echoed through the deep (Ezek. 43:2; Rev. 1:15; 14:2). As He spoke, light gushed out from His divine lips and pierced through the vast expanse of utter darkness. The angelic hosts clapped their hands in adoration as the light swallowed up the darkness. They shouted for joy and praised the Most High God (Job 38:7). With their faces to the ground in worship to the King of Kings and Lord of Lords, the angelic hosts cried out "Holy, holy, holy is the LORD Almighty; the whole earth is full of his glory" (Isa. 6:3 NIV)

For five incredible days, the angelic hosts had the enviable privilege of watching Elohim bring the universe into existence, separate the waters into clouds and oceans, and isolate the dry land. It was their singular honor to observe God speak into existence all types of vegetation. They watched in amazement as God created different species of aquatic and terrestrial animals and called forth the planetary system and the galaxies. To their utter amazement, God assigned functions to each one of His creations and set boundaries to their spheres of operation. The angelic hosts were further fascinated to see God put reproductive seed in every organism He created to ensure that His created beings would be capable of reproducing after their unique kind.

On the sixth day, the LORD God set out to fashion His masterpiece. This would be the most outstanding of all His created works. When the angels heard the triune God discuss this plan, they were perplexed, to say the least. They had always thought they were the crown of God's creation. Though unsure about what God was up to, the angels understood that the Sovereign God reserved the right to do whatever He liked, however He liked it, and did not need to consult anyone before embarking on any venture.

Wanting His masterpiece to be like Him, God visualized a unique species of creatures that would be triune in nature. These creatures would be the exact reflection of Him in terms of glory,

*The Holy Spirit*

power, and majesty. They would exercise dominion on earth on God's behalf and rule over all His creation on earth.

With this clear picture in mind, God took moist clay from the earth, meticulously formed a skeletal structure for support, and covered it with muscles and layers of skin lined with nerve endings. He carefully created nearly thirty-eight trillion cells, joined them to form tissues, and grouped them into various organs. God then linked specific organs together into systems to perform the functions He had predetermined for them to perform. For one system, he assigned the responsibility of respiration; to one, digestion; to another, excretion; and yet to another, reproduction. He also fashioned systems that would collect and process sensory and chemical information throughout the body and circulate blood around the body. When everything was in place as He wanted, God closed the creature up. There he lay on the ground—naked and lifeless.

Then the LORD God stooped over the lifeless creature, put His divine lips on the lips of clay and His glorious nose on the nose of clay, and released a heavy dose of His Spirit into the man's nostrils. Immediately, a gentle explosion was heard, and the Spirit of God released the nature of God into the man. Instantly, breath began to flow through the man's respiratory system, and blood began streaming through his veins and arteries as the Spirit of God impacted life to the man's organs and systems.

Thus, the man became a living being! He became self-conscious. His intellect, emotions, and senses suddenly began to function. When he opened his eyes, his gaze met that of his Maker. He returned God's infectious smile. God reached out His powerful right hand and helped the man to his feet. There he stood, looking exactly as God had pictured. God's masterpiece! He was flawless! He looked excellent! God called the man Adam because he (the man) was made from the earth (from the Hebrew *adama* meaning earth).

One day, while Adam was sleeping, God formed a female from a rib He had taken from Adam. Adam could hardly believe his eyes when he woke up from his deep sleep and saw her. Stunned by her presence and mesmerized by her indescribable beauty, he declared, "This at last is bone of my bones and flesh of my flesh; she shall be called Woman, because she was taken out of Man" (Gen. 2:23 ESV).

**Unmasking the Account**

**God Revealed in His Creation**

When you read the creation account as recorded in the first two chapters of Genesis, and from the writings of Isaiah, David, and other prophets, you cannot help but conclude that humans are the height of all that God created. Human beings are God's masterpiece! Now, that is a staggering thought, especially when we consider the wonder of other great creations such as the magnificence and awesome power of angels, the force of the oceans, and the wonder of the galaxies.

Think about this for a moment. A galaxy is a system of billions of stars held together by gravitational attraction. The observable universe is believed to contain hundreds of billions of galaxies with varying morphologies. Even with the use of the most sophisticated instruments, astrophysicists have yet to discover all there is to these incredibly wonderful heavenly bodies. God, in His infinite wisdom, has assigned the galaxies the function of declaring His glory (Ps. 19:1). Without speech, the galaxies faithfully declare the goodness of God (Ps. 19:2–6).

> The heavens declare the glory of God; the skies proclaim the work of his hands. Day after day they pour forth speech; night after night they reveal knowledge. They have no speech, they use no words; no sound is heard from them. Yet their voice goes out into all the earth, their words to the ends of the world. In the heavens God has pitched a

tent for the sun. It is like a bridegroom coming out of his chamber, like a champion rejoicing to run his course. It rises at one end of the heavens and makes its circuit to the other; nothing is deprived of its warmth. (Ps. 19:1–6 NIV)

The entire creation testifies to God's invisible qualities—His eternal power and divine nature (Rom. 1:20).

For ever since the world was created, people have seen the earth and sky. Through everything God made, they can clearly see his invisible qualities—his eternal power and divine nature. So they have no excuse for not knowing God. (Rom. 1:20 NLT)

Angels stand in the very presence of God and offer Him unceasing worship. They also execute God's will in heaven and on earth. As God's messengers, they have been created with incredible power, which they exercise on God's behalf. Despite these, humanity alone has been assigned the singular honor of being called God's image and reflector of God's likeness. That makes us God's highest creative work—God's masterpiece! We are God's masterpiece (Eph. 2:10 NLT).

## The Indispensable Role of the Holy Spirit in Creation

Often lost in the account of creation is the indispensable role the Holy Spirit played in bringing the universe into existence and in the creation of humans. Each person of the triune God played an active role in creation. While it is easy to appreciate the role of God the Father and that of God the Son (God's Word) in the creation account, the vital role of the Holy Spirit is often glossed over. The fact is, the Holy Spirit played an indispensable role in creation.

First, the Holy Spirit activated the creative, spoken Word of the Father to bring the heavens (galaxies) and the earth into existence.

Second, it took the awesome power of the Holy Spirit to transform the dark, formless, chaotic universe into an orderly one. Third, the Holy Spirit activated the hand of the Father as He placed the planets in their orbits and assigned the sun, moon, and hundreds of billions of stars to their designated spheres. Fourth, the Holy Spirit impacted life to man. When Adam was created, he was lifeless until the Father breathed into his nostrils the breath (Spirit) of life. That explosive breath of life from the nostrils of God was the Holy Spirit. Thus, it was the Holy Spirit, who gave life to man and made him a living soul!

This truth is reiterated in Job 33:4: "The Spirit of God has made me; the breath of the Almighty gives me life" (NIV). Earlier in Job 27:3, the Bible explains that we can enjoy the gift of life only as long as the breath (Spirit) of God remains in us. In Psalm 104:30, the Bible declares we were created when God sent forth His Spirit. Our continual spiritual existence is directly linked to our connectedness to the Holy Spirit. When we cut ourselves off from the Holy Spirit, we lose our vital source of spiritual supply. The apostle James affirms this truth when he wrote "the body *without the spirit* is dead" (James 2:26 NIV, emphasis mine). Living without the Holy Spirit is spiritual death because the Holy Spirit is our indispensable source of spiritual life.

> **Remember**
>
> *Living without the Holy Spirit is spiritual death because the Holy Spirit is our indispensable source of spiritual life.*

What sets you apart from all other creatures is that you have a part of God residing in you. You are partly heavenly and partly earthly. This unique nature makes you the only creature capable of relating to God and the earth simultaneously. You are created in the image (reflection) and likeness (resemblance) of God (Gen. 1:27). One way in which you resemble God is that you are triune in nature just like God. God is Father, Son, and the Holy Spirit, and you are spirit, soul, and body (1 Thess. 5:23). No other creature has this unique characteristic.

With your body, you can relate to your world through your five senses. With your soul, you are conscious of yourself through your intellect, will, and emotions. With your spirit, you are capable of relating to your Creator and offering Him worship. Just as the first man had to receive God's breath (Spirit) to become a living being, you need the Holy Spirit to live the kind of life God intended you to live. Additionally, just as God's breath (Spirit) was indispensable for the first man to operate as God had designed him to, you certainly need the Holy Spirit to fulfill your God-ordained purpose for your life.

## The Holy Spirit Sustains the Universe

The Holy Spirit played an indispensable role in the creation of the universe (Gen. 1:2), and He plays an equally indispensable role in the efficient running of the universe. A conscientious study of the Bible shows that the Holy Spirit is actively involved in the orderly functioning of the universe. For example, the Holy Spirit (together with Father God and the Son) carefully calculates how much dust should be in a particular location, weighs mountains and hills to determine their suitability at their location, and measures the amount of water bodies that should exist in various parts of the universe. Undoubtedly, this intricate work of the Holy Spirit is beyond our understanding, but the Holy Spirit graciously inspired Isaiah to paint a little picture of it for us.

> Who has measured the waters in the hollow of His hand, and marked off the heavens with a span [of the hand], and calculated the dust of the earth with a measure, and weighed the mountains in a balance and the hills in a pair of scales? Who has directed the Spirit of the Lord, or has taught Him as His counselor? (Isaiah 40:12–13 AMP)

Another ongoing ministry of the Holy Spirit is the adornment of the universe with beauty. Long before anyone ever thought about inventing astronomical instruments, the Bible had inspired the writer of Job to make the following declaration: "By His Spirit He adorned the heavens" (Job 26:13 NKJV). By His Spirit, God adorned and continues to adorn the universe with beauty and majesty. The continuing beauty of the heavenly bodies and their incredible maneuvers, and the wonders of the oceans are mere edges of His ways and small whispers of Him (Job 26:14 NKJV).

Thanks to the invention of highly sophisticated telescopes and cameras, we can now "spoil" ourselves with the amazements of the universe. The Holy Spirit also preserves and renews creation. This truth is beautifully stated in Psalm 104:30: When You send Your Spirit, they are created, and You renew the face of the earth (NIV). Since all the above stated activities are the works of God, they also attest to the divinity of the Holy Spirit

## God's Purpose for You

God's purpose for creating you is for Him to have a personal relationship with you just as a Father relates to the child he loves. The only appropriate way of relating to God is with your spirit and in truth (John 4:23–24). It's important for you to realize that God made you in such a way as to depend on Him to be complete. Remember when God breathed into man, he became a living soul. In the Hebrew, the word for soul means an entity that depends on another.

As long as Adam depended on God, he reigned as king over God's creation. However, when he decided to dispense of God, he became a slave of Satan. In the same way, you can live your God-ordained, abundant life if and only if you learn to depend on God the Holy Spirit to lead, teach, and guide you. He is your indispensable source of life. Once your relationship with the Holy Spirit is right, your soul (will, intellect, and emotions) will line up with God's plan and purpose for your life. Your body will then move according to the dictates of the Holy Spirit working through your spirit and soul to execute the greater works Jesus promised you will do (John 14:12).

Is anything out of order in your life? Is insecurity, fear of the unknown, or threats from within and without draining faith out of your life? Remember the Holy Spirit brings order to chaotic situations, gives life to lifeless beings, and brings hope to hopeless circumstances. If you need restoration to a place of spiritual fruitfulness, your answer is the Holy Spirit. All you need to do is to tap into His fullness by asking Him to be your personal helper. You can't do without Him. Remember He's on earth to help you achieve your God-ordained purpose. The good news is that He's only a prayer away. He's waiting for your call. Will you call Him right now for His indispensable help?

**Tapping into the Story**

God invites you to the realm of supernatural living. Just as God lifted Adam up after He stooped down to breath into his nostrils, He wants to lift you up unto the supernatural plane after He has stooped down to recreate you. The Christian life is a supernatural life. It is not meant to be lived in the natural or with natural ability. The door to this supernatural life is the new birth. If you have not experienced it but desire to, simply pray this prayer in faith:

> Dear God, I thank you that you love me and you want me to be your child. I acknowledge that I am a sinner, living under the weight of your just penalty. I also acknowledge that you sent your only beloved Son Jesus to pay the penalty for my sin when He died on the cross. For this, I thank you. Now, God, I am sorry for my sinful lifestyle. I repent of my sin. I want to begin a new life with you. Please send your Holy Spirit to live in me to

> help me live a life that pleases you. Thank you for your answered prayer. Amen.

If you prayed that prayer faithfully, your spirit has been recreated. You have received the new birth. In other words, you have been born again. On the other hand, if you are already born again, you need to acknowledge that the Holy Spirit is indispensable in every aspect of your life. It takes the Holy Spirit to bring meaning and order to your life. Where there is chaos, He creates order and tranquility. He alone can turn the listless situations in your life into productive ones. He is ready to help you exchange every hopeless situation in your life for abundant, fruitful living.

Your life can only become complete if you yield to the Lordship of the Holy Spirit and allow Him to live and work through you (2 Cor. 3:17). If you allow the Holy Spirit to have His rightful place in your life, you will not be like a ship being tossed to and fro on a turbulent ocean; instead, you will be like a fruitful vine that brings its fruits in its seasons (Ps. 1:3).

# PART II

## The Holy Spirit: Who Is He—and Why Is He Indispensable?

## Chapter 3

### Indispensable Characteristics I

*Dispensing of or underutilizing the ministry of the Holy Spirit will, without a doubt, make us less effective in our God-ordained callings.*

ROGER MILLA MADE HIS mark on the international scene at the twilight of his professional career. At age thirty-eight, when most soccer players hung up their boots, Milla secured a niche for himself in the Cameroonian National Team during the 1990 FIFA World Cup in Italy, as one player the team could not do without. His four incredible goals against some of the tournament's favorite teams helped Cameroon become the first African nation to reach the quarterfinal stage of the competition. As if that was not enough, four years later, during the 1994 FIFA World Cup held in the United States, Milla made history again when at age forty-three years, he scored against Russia to become the oldest goal scorer in any World Cup. Roger Milla's role in the Cameroonian national soccer team can aptly be described as indispensable!

We use the word *indispensable* to describe somebody whose role in a team is absolutely necessary or essential. Typically, we describe somebody as indispensable if the person plays such an important role that their team cannot do without them. An indispensable person cannot be replaced or dispensed of without the team suffering some loss.

Sports organizations spend huge sums of money on athletes they consider indispensable. In August 2017, Neymar de Santos Junior became the highest-paid soccer player in the world when Paris Saint-Germain (PSG) of France agreed to pay him $350 million in salary and bonus.[1] If transfer fees and other service fees are added, PSG will spend more than $600 million on Neymar in five years. Why would the French club spend such a huge sum of money on one player? The answer is not far-fetched. Neymar has exceptional skills and capabilities. He is he slick on the ball, is an excellent distributor of balls, and can set up strikers to score goals. Most importantly, Neymar is a terrific goal scorer. In a nutshell, Neymar is the epitome of an indispensable player. Obviously, the leadership of PSG understood that no matter the cost paid to purchase a player of Neymar's caliber, the benefit from the purchase would greatly outweigh the cost. An indispensable personality cannot be measured by its "price."

The purpose of this chapter and the next is to provide an overview of the indispensable characteristics of the Holy Spirit and answer two important questions: Who is the Holy Spirit—and why is the Holy Spirit indispensable? We will answer the first question within the context of "divine mystery" and the second question in terms of the names, unique personality, divine attributes, divine works, and the symbols of the Holy Spirit as found in scripture.

---

[1] https://www.forbes.com/sites/christinasettimi/2017/08/03/neymar-set-to-eclipse-messi-and-ronaldo-and-become-the-worlds-highest-paid-soccer-player/#11b074811912

## Indispensability of the Holy Spirit: Overview

The Bible is replete with passages that point to the indispensability of the Holy Spirit. But for the instrumentality of the Holy Spirit, the universe and the human race would not have been created (Gen. 1:2; Job 33:4), the Bible would not have been written (2 Pet. 1:21),

> **Remember**
>
> *God never intended us to live without the Holy Spirit.*

salvation would not have been possible (Titus 3:5), and Christians would not have power to be effective witnesses of Jesus Christ (Acts 1:8). The Holy Spirit is indispensable for living the kind of life that pleases God and for fulfilling our God-ordained assignments on earth. In fact, God never intended us to live without the Holy Spirit.

After creating the first man (Adam) in His own image and likeness, Adam lay lifeless in the dust. It was only after *God breathed His Spirit* into Adam that that he became a *living* being (or soul). In other words, it was the Holy Spirit who impacted life to man; therefore, man's continuing existence depended on the presence of the Holy Spirit in him. When man disobeyed God's command not to eat from the tree of the knowledge of good and evil, God effected the promise He had made to man: "On the day you eat from it (the tree of the knowledge of good and evil), you will certainly die" (Gen. 2:17 CEV).

Thus, when man fell as a result of disobedience to God's command, he lost the spiritual component that God had impacted to him when He breathed into him at creation. Adam (and for that matter the human race) lost the presence of the Holy Spirit and thus died—spiritually. Though Adam and Eve continued to live for several hundreds of years after the fall, the process of decay was set in motion the moment they sinned.

I will elaborate more on this in the subsequent chapters but suffice it now to say that the fall of man is a strong pointer to the indispensability of the Holy Spirit in the life of man. How? At creation, man received life only after God had breathed His Spirit into man and the moment man sinned, he lost the presence of the Holy Spirit and so died—first spiritually and later physically.

Since the fall, God has been working through the events of human history to bring humankind back to Himself. In other words, God has been working through human history to restore to man the presence of the Holy Spirit. God desires a personal relationship with humankind through His Spirit, and He has not allowed anything to stop His plan. Sin and Satan sometimes delayed or even stalled God's plan temporarily but ultimately, God has ensured that only His purposes were accomplished—in His time! The quest of the ages, therefore, is God seeking to breathe into man once again the indispensable Holy Spirit, without whom man has no spiritual life.

Again, to demonstrate to us that we cannot do anything of value for the Lord, God never used anyone without first filling him with His Holy Spirit. I will throw more light on this in the next two chapters. Finally, when God took on human form in the person of Jesus, He made sure that every aspect of Jesus's life was empowered by the Holy Spirit. Jesus was conceived by the Holy Spirit (Matt. 1:18), was anointed by the Holy Spirit for His unparallel earthly ministry (Acts 10:31), and was resurrected from death by the Holy Spirit (Rom. 8:11). The fact that Jesus needed the Holy Spirit in every aspect of His life attests to the indispensability of the Holy Spirit for victorious living and effective ministry.

Jesus underscores the indispensable role the Holy Spirit plays in our lives:

> *Remember*
>
> *The quest of the ages is God seeking to breathe into man once again the indispensable Holy Spirit, without whom man has no spiritual life.*

> Nevertheless, I tell you the truth: *It is expedient for you* that I go away: for if I go not away, the Comforter will not come unto you; but if I depart, I will send him unto you. (John 16:7 KJV, emphasis mine)

The word *expedient* means advantageous, useful, helpful, or beneficial. Thus, Jesus is saying, "It is to your advantage that I go away" (ESV), "It is to your benefit that I go away" (Berean Study Bible), or "It is best for you that I go away" (NLT).

Whatever way one looks at it, it is clear in this passage that Jesus is assuring His disciples that as important as His presence with them is, the presence of the Holy Spirit with them would be more beneficial. Think about that for a minute. If Jesus *had* to make way for the Holy Spirit to come, then the presence of the Holy Spirit in our lives must be indispensable. While on earth, Jesus could be in only one place at a time. However, with the Holy Spirit residing in every believer, Jesus can perform His works multiple times over everywhere in the world at the same time. This is why He says it is best for us that He goes away.

God expects us to relate to the Holy Spirit as we would to Jesus. In some sense, the Holy Spirit is Jesus residing inside us in another form. Just as we cannot do without Jesus, neither can we do without the Holy Spirit (John 15:5).

## The Mystery of the Holy Spirit

In everyday language, a mystery is understood to be something that is difficult or even impossible to comprehend or explain or something that is so obscure that even if it is unfolded, it will not be understood. When the Bible uses the word *mystery*, however, it refers to God's secret plan (or truth)

> **Remember**
>
> *Just as we cannot do without Jesus, neither can we do without the Holy Spirit.*

that He graciously reveals to His covenanted people. In this sense, a mystery is truth that is hidden from people who are outside of God's covenant but are made known to those who have a covenant relationship with God. Examples of mysteries in the Bible are the mystery of the Gospel (1 Cor. 1:18), the mystery of marriage (Eph. 5:32), the relationship between Christ and His Church (Eph. 1:22–23; 5:32), godliness (1 Tim. 3:16), and Christian stewardship (1 Cor. 4:2).

Perhaps the greatest mystery that unfolds in the Bible right from Genesis all the way to Revelation is the truth that God is one and yet He exists as more than one person. This doctrine is generally referred to as the Holy Trinity. In simple terms, the doctrine of the Trinity is the scriptural truth that God is one in substance, equal in power and glory but manifested in three persons: the Father, Son, and Holy Spirit. The scriptures that affirm this truth include 1 John 5:7; Matthew 28:19; 2 Corinthians 13:14; Exodus 3:14; John 14:11; 1 Corinthians 8:6; John 1:14, 18; and 15:26; and Galatians 4:6.

While a full discourse of the doctrine of the Trinity will demand another book, suffice it to say that as the third person of the Trinity, the Holy Spirit is coequal with the Father and the Son (Jesus) in substance and divine attributes but distinct in functions. In the rest of this chapter, we will discuss the personality of the Holy Spirit, the marvelous names and titles ascribed to Him, His divine attributes, and the symbols used to describe Him in scripture and their meanings. The goal is to establish the indispensability of the Holy Spirit and learn how we can develop an intimate relationship with Him.

## Personality of the Holy Spirit

Lots of well-meaning Christians perceive the Holy Spirit as some kind of irresistible static electric energy that causes people to do unusual things. Others believe the Holy Spirit is just a powerful force that comes on people and makes them shake, scream, or fall. It is common to hear some ministers ascribe their inability to operate within their assigned time to the Holy Spirit, implying that the Holy Spirit is either undisciplined or makes people do things against their will. The aforementioned perceptions beg the questions, "Is the Holy Spirit a person or a force—and what roles does the Holy Spirit play in the life of the believer?"

## Is the Holy Spirit a Person or a Force?

In answering this question, it is important to explain the difference between a person and a force. A person is a *being* that has the ability to exercise the power of self-consciousness and self-determination. A person has the capacity to express their thoughts and reveal their will through what they say or do and the intelligible emotions they express. In other words, a person can think, speak, *and* express emotions such as anger, hurt, and happiness. A force, on the other hand, is *something* that can cause a stationary object to move or a moving body to move faster, slower, or stop.

The next important fact to underscore is that the New Testament was originally written in Greek (mainly) and later translated into various languages. Now, in the Greek New Testament text, the personality of the Holy Spirit is uniquely portrayed in terms of both the personal gender "He" and the neuter gender "it." Moreover, the definite article "the" precedes the name of the Holy Spirit in some cases, and "the" is omitted in other instances. This distinction may not be obvious when reading the Bible in English and other languages (different from Greek). In the English translations, the translators inserted the definite article "the" throughout the text to fit English language grammar usage.

Also in the Greek text, wherever the phrase "the Holy Spirit" is used, it is followed by the personal pronoun "He," depicting the Holy Spirit as a person. However, wherever "Holy Spirit" is used, it is followed by the neuter pronoun "it," signifying the influence the Holy Spirit exerts in the situation rather than as person. The Holy Spirit (as impersonal influence) can manifest Himself as a glory cloud, fire, rushing wind or as a cool, sweet, assuring presence.

As person, the Holy Spirit appointed and sent out leaders, gave directions, and can be blasphemed. For example, in Acts 13:1 – 2, the Holy Spirit spoke clearly to the leaders of the church at Antioch and gave them specific instructions to "set apart ... Barnabas and Saul" for a special ministry.

> **13** ¹ Now in the church at Antioch there were prophets and teachers: Barnabas, Simeon called Niger, Lucius of Cyrene, Manaen (who had been brought up with Herod the tetrarch) and Saul. ²While they (the teachers and prophets at Antioch) were worshiping the Lord and fasting, *the Holy Spirit said*, "Set apart for me Barnabas and Saul for the work to which I have called them." (Acts 13:1 – 2 NIV, emphasis mine)

The ability to speak is a distinctive personality trait. Thus, in this passage, the Holy Spirit, as *person*, appointed Barnabas and Paul for the first missionary journey. Only a person can give orders and assign responsibilities to leaders.

When the Jewish leaders accused Jesus of casting out demons by the power of Beelzebub (chief of demons), Jesus said:

> Anyone who speaks a word against the Son of Man will be forgiven, but anyone who speaks against the Holy Spirit will not be forgiven, either in this age or in the age to come. (Matt. 12:32 NIV)

In this passage, Jesus contrasts the consequences of speaking blasphemies against Him (as Person) and speaking blasphemies against the Holy Spirit (as Person).

When faced with the question of whether to subject non-Jewish believers to Jewish religious practices, the apostles made a resolution at the Jerusalem Council not to burden non-Jewish people with Jewish ceremonial laws but to ask non-Jewish Christians to abstain from food offered to idols, sexual immorality, and strangled meat. They also made the following statement:

*The Holy Spirit*

> It seemed good *to the Holy Spirit* (Person) and *to us* (Persons) not to burden you with anything beyond the following requirements. (Acts 15:28 NIV, emphasis mine)

It is clear, in this passage, that the apostles acknowledged the Holy Spirit as *Person* who related to them as *persons*.

In contrast, the New Testament uses "Holy Spirit" when the Holy Spirit overshadows, fills, or anoints people. As stated earlier, you will not notice the omission of "the" if you are reading the English Bible because the translators inserted "the" in front of "Holy Spirit" to conform to normal English language usage. Here are some examples:

- And with that he breathed on them and said, "Receive *Holy Spirit*" (John 20:22 NIV, emphasis mine).
- "For John baptized in water, but in a few days, you will be baptized in *Holy Spirit*" (Acts 1:5 NIV, emphasis mine)
- "How God anointed Jesus of Nazareth with *Holy Spirit* and power, and how he went around doing good and healing all who were under the power of the devil, because God was with him" (Act 10:38 NIV, emphasis mine).
- "The kingdom of God is … righteousness and peace and joy in *Holy Ghost*" (Rom. 14:17 KJV).

In a nutshell, the Holy Spirit is a Person. However, whenever He exerts His influence on a situation or a person, He manifests Himself as a Presence.

### Personality Marks of the Holy Spirit

As stated earlier, the distinctive characteristics of a person includes the ability to think, speak, make

> **Remember**
>
> *The Holy Spirit is a person. However, whenever He exerts His influence in a situation or a person, He manifests Himself as a presence.*

decisions, and express emotions. The following are some of the personality traits the Holy Spirit exhibits in scripture.

## I: The Holy Spirit Has a Mind

The Bible reveals that the Holy Spirit has a mind and a will, which He expresses through speech and intelligible emotions. For example, in Romans 8:26, the Bible tells us that we don't know how to pray as we ought to, but the Holy Spirit prays through us with groaning too deep for words to express. Only a person with intelligence can help us pray. Then in the next verse, the Bible says this:

> *Remember*
>
> *The Bible makes it clear that the Holy Spirit has a mind and a will, which He expresses through speech and intelligible emotions.*

> And he who searches our hearts knows the mind of the Spirit, because the Spirit intercedes for God's people in accordance with the will of God. (Rom. 8:27 NIV, emphasis mine)

Here, the Bible shows us two characteristics of the Holy Spirit:
The Holy Spirit *has a mind* and, the Holy Spirit *can intercede* for us.
The word intercede means to act as a mediator or advocate. Obviously, the Holy Spirit would not be able to intercede for the saints if He did not have a mind.
Also, in 1 Corinthians 2:9–13, the Bible explicitly declares that the Holy Spirit has a mind and can act intelligibly:

> What no eye has seen, what no ear has heard, and what no human mind has conceived the things God has prepared for those who love him these

are the things God has revealed to us by his Spirit. The Spirit searches all things, even the deep things of God. For who knows a person's thoughts except their own spirit within them? In the same way no one knows the thoughts of God except the Spirit of God. What we have received is not the spirit of the world, but the Spirit who is from God, so that we may understand what God has freely given us. This is what we speak, not in words taught us by human wisdom but in words taught by the Spirit, explaining spiritual realities with Spirit-taught words. (1 Cor. 2:9–13 NIV, emphasis mine)

From this passage of scripture, we can clearly see that the Holy Spirit demonstrates explicit characteristics of personality including the ability to search the deep, hidden things of God, knowing the thoughts of God, teaching, and explaining spiritual realities. Only a person with a mind and the ability to act intelligibly can do these things.

Jesus gave His disciples the following promise concerning the Holy Spirit:

> But the Advocate, the Holy Spirit, whom the Father will send in my name, will teach you all things and will remind you of everything I have said to you. (John 14:26 NIV)

Again, only a person can teach. The Holy Spirit has to be a person to be able to teach the disciples "all" things and remind them of "everything" Jesus had taught them. In effect, Jesus was telling the disciples "the Holy Spirit will teach you everything you need to know and will remind you of all that I have taught." I never cease to be amazed by the degree of remembrance the Holy Spirit brought to the disciples. How else could they remember all that Jesus did and said except the Holy Spirit was their special remembrancer?

The Holy Spirit is still the teacher of what we need to know and the remembrancer of all that Jesus wants us to understand. It is important for us, as believers, to constantly acknowledge our need for the teaching and reminding ministries of the Holy Spirit in our lives. Jesus said it is profitable that He went away so the Holy Spirit would come and teach us *all* that we need to know. Are you battled by life's challenges or faced with distressing issues of life? Please call upon the Holy Spirit to teach you what you must do. As your indwelling helper, He may choose to speak directly to your spirit or through the pages of scriptures. He will give you a specific message tailored to meet your present need.

## II: The Holy Spirit Has a Will

In 1 Corinthians 12:11, we are told the Holy Spirit has a will. He distributes gifts to each and every believer as He wills. It is not up to us to determine which gifts to operate in. That is the prerogative of the Holy Spirit. The Bible commands us to earnestly desire the more excellent gifts (1 Cor. 12:31), but the Holy Spirit reserves the right to give us the gifts He wants to give us. Hebrews 2:4 confirms that the Holy Spirit gives us gifts according to His own will. "God also testified to it by signs, wonders and various miracles, and by gifts of the Holy Spirit distributed according to His will" (Heb. 2:4 ESV, emphasis mine).

## III: The Holy Spirit Speaks

As would be expected of a person, the Holy Spirit speaks. This is beautifully illustrated in Acts 8:29: "Then the Spirit said to Philip, 'Go near and overtake this chariot'" (NKJV). Also, in Acts 10:19–20, the Holy Spirit spoke to Peter:

> Behold, three men are seeking you. Arise therefore, go down and go with them, doubting nothing; for I have sent them. (NKJV)

Again, as I mentioned earlier, while the leaders of the church at Antioch were fasting and ministering to the Lord, the Holy Spirit called Barnabas and Saul unto special foreign missions.

> Now in the church that was at Antioch there were certain prophets and teachers: Barnabas, Simeon who was called Niger, Lucius of Cyrene, Manaen who had been brought up with Herod the tetrarch, and Saul. As they ministered to the Lord and fasted, the Holy Spirit said, *"Now separate to Me Barnabas and Saul for the work to which I have called them."* (Acts 13:1–2 NKJV, emphasis mine)

Only a person can call these leaders unto apostolic ministry. The authoritative tone of the last part of verse 2, "Now separate to Me Barnabas and Saul for the work to which I have called them," suggests that the speaker (the Holy Spirit) was a divine person.

### IV: The Holy Spirit Makes Strategic Decisions

In Acts 16:6–7, the Holy Spirit demonstrated another personhood attribute. He prohibited Paul and his entourage from proceeding on their originally planned route. On two occasions, the Holy Spirit did not permit them to resume their planned journey.

> Now when they had gone through Phrygia and the region of Galatia, they were forbidden by the Holy Spirit to preach the word in Asia. After they had come to Mysia, they tried to go into Bithynia, but the Spirit did not permit them. So passing by Mysia, they came down to Troas. And a vision appeared to Paul in the night. A man of Macedonia stood and pleaded with him, saying, "Come over to Macedonia and help us." Now after he had seen the vision, immediately we sought to go to Macedonia,

> concluding that the Lord had called us to preach the gospel to them. (Acts 16:6–10 NKJV)

Paul and his team of missionaries were repeatedly prohibited by the Holy Spirit from preaching the Gospel in Asia, which was close to the region where they were. The Spirit, however, led them to preach in the continent of Europe. Historic events show how strategic this move of the Holy Spirit was for the spread of the Gospel. Since its inception in Europe, Christianity has been the dominant force in Western civilization, exerting significant influence on Western education, philosophy, science, and art. Europe also became the springboard for the spread of Christianity to North and South America, Africa, and Asia. It all became possible when the Holy Spirit made the strategic decision to direct Paul and his apostolic team to the continent of Europe.

## V: The Holy Spirit Can Show Emotions

Another personality trait the Holy Spirit shows is intelligible emotions. In Ephesians 4:30, we are admonished "not to grieve the Holy Spirit of God" (NIV). We grieve or make the Holy Spirit sad when we let unwholesome talk come out of our mouths and allow "bitterness, rage and anger, brawling and slander, along with every form of malice" have the better of us (Eph. 4:29, 31 NIV). When the Israelites "rebelled and grieved God's Holy Spirit, He turned and became their enemy and He himself fought against them" (Isa. 63:10 NIV). Obviously, a force cannot be rebelled against or grieved; only a person can be grieved, and only an authority personality can be rebelled against. In His stern warning to people who commit apostasy, the writer of the Epistle to the Hebrews said:

> Just think how much worse the punishment will be for those who have trampled on the Son of God, and have treated the blood of the covenant, which made us holy, as if it were common and unholy,

> and have *insulted and disdained* the Holy Spirit who brings God's mercy to us. (Heb. 10:29 NLT, emphasis mine)

We see from this passage that the Holy Spirit is a divine person (together with Jesus and the Father) who can be insulted and treated with contempt. The Son of God shed His holy blood to make salvation available to us, and the Holy Spirit brings the mercy and grace of God to us. So, if a person accepts this grace of God and then later renounces it, he rejects the person (the Holy Spirit) who *alone* can avail the grace of God to him. Such a person blasphemes the Holy Spirit and our Lord Jesus Christ warns that anyone who blasphemes against the Holy Spirit will not be forgiven.

> And so I tell you, every kind of sin and slander can be forgiven, but blasphemy against the Spirit will not be forgiven. Anyone who speaks a word against the Son of Man will be forgiven, but anyone who speaks against the Holy Spirit will not be forgiven, either in this age or in the age to come. (Matt. 12:31–32 NIV)

Blasphemy means to insult a deity or treat a deity with contempt or irreverence. Jesus affirms the deity of the Holy Spirit in the above passage and sternly warns against blasphemy against the Holy Spirit. Since the Holy Spirit is the divine person who helps us to accept God's mercy and grace, we must accord Him the reverence He deserves.

Another way by which we know the Holy Spirit has feelings is that scripture commands us not to quench the Holy Spirit:

> Do not quench the Spirit. Do not despise prophecies. Test all things; hold fast what is good. (1 Thess. 5:19–21 NKJV)

The word *quench* means to douse or put out fire. We quench the Holy Spirit if we try to suppress Him from manifesting His gifts through us or others. A special mention is made of the gift of prophecy because it is the spiritual gift God uses to speak to His people directly. God warns us not to despise (treat with contempt or look down upon) prophecy (or spiritual gifts in general) because that amounts to despising the Holy Spirit who gives the gift(s). It is important to remember that the Lord honors those who honor Him but lightly esteems those who despise Him (1 Sam. 2:30). To maintain balance and order, however, saints are admonished to "test" the authenticity of spiritual gifts (by the standard of the Written Word) and retain aspects of prophetic utterances that are consistent with scripture.

## VI: The Holy Spirit Can Be Lied To

Another attribute that illustrates that the Holy Spirit is a person is that He can be lied to. In Acts chapter 5, a man named Ananias and his wife, Sapphira, conspired to deceive the first-century apostles but the Holy Spirit quickly revealed their deceit to Peter and the following ensued:

> Then Peter said, "Ananias, how is it that Satan has so filled your heart that *you have lied to the Holy Spirit* and have kept for yourself some of the money you received for the land? ... *You have not lied just to human beings but to God.*" (Acts 5:3–4 NIV, emphasis mine)

It is very instructive to learn here that lying to God's human representatives amounts to lying to God the Holy Spirit Himself. It fulfills Jesus's promise that He would return to them in another form and that He would be with them till the end of age (John 14:18; Matt. 28:20). Other indispensable characteristics of the Holy Spirit are discussed in the next chapter.

## Chapter Takeaway

God did not ordain the Christian life to be lived without the Holy Spirit.

- We cannot be all that God ordained us to be without the Holy Spirit.
- Our effectiveness as Christians depends on our relationship with the Holy Spirit.
- The unique characteristics of the Holy Spirit affirm His indispensability.

## Personal Challenge

In this chapter, we have discussed seven personality traits of the Holy Spirit. During the next seven days, reflect on one characteristic each day and ask God to help you get to know the Holy Spirit experientially as your indispensable friend. You may use the template below for this exercise:

Day #1: Monday, July 28, 2018
Characteristic of the Holy Spirit:
_____
_____

My personal reflection on this characteristic:
_____
_____
_____
_____
_____
_____
_____

## Chapter 4

### Indispensable Characteristics II

*Just as human attorneys stand in court with their clients, the Holy Spirit stands with us through thick and thin, assuring us that we are covered.*

IN THE BIBLE, NAMES have special significance. Names are given for identification, and they signify the character and sometimes functions of the person who bears the name. For example, Jesus gave Simon (meaning obedient servant) the name "Peter" (meaning rock) to signify Simon's God-ordained fortitude and stability of character. Similarly, in the Old Testament, God changed the names of Abram (meaning exalted father) to Abraham (meaning father of many nations) and Jacob (meaning usurper) to Israel (meaning prince of God) to indicate the unique functions and character God had ordained for them.

In the same way, the Bible ascribes names and titles to the Holy Spirit to indicate the diverse, indispensable roles the Holy Spirit plays in our lives. There are at least thirty-five names for the Holy Spirit identified in scripture. In this chapter, I will discuss seven of these names to illustrate the indispensability of the Holy Spirit. I encourage you to spend some time meditating on each one of them, and as you do so, I pray that the Holy Spirit will create in you a fresh longing for a deeper, more intimate relationship with Him as your personal, indispensable friend.

**Titles and Names of the Holy Spirit**

**I: Comforter or Advocate**

In John 14:16–17; 15:26; and 16:7, Jesus refers to the Holy Spirit as the Comforter. This is perhaps the most well-known title of the Holy Spirit. The Greek word translated Comforter is Parakletos, from which we get the English transliteration Paraclete, which means "One called to the side of another." In ancient Greece, a Paraclete was a person who ran alongside an exhausted marathon athlete, to encourage the athlete not to give up and to assure him/her that the prize was in sight. Paraclete also means strengthener, helper, encourager, or legal counselor. As the Christian's Paraclete, the Holy Spirit encourages us; He motivates us to keep keeping on, and He provides us with the strength we need to run the faith race.

Through the changing scenes of my life, I have experienced the Holy Spirit as my indispensable helper. In the early part of 2003, I was going through a very discouraging situation in my life. For three consecutive years, I gained admission to a Bible college in a neighboring country, but the top official in my denomination—who was designated to provide me with the recommendation I needed—refused to sign my recommendation letter simply because I did not obtain my diploma in theology from our denomination. Ironically, he had signed recommendation letters for other people in my situation and even people who were not members of our denomination.

When I went to church the Sunday after the third rejection, I felt like an outcast—unwanted, dejected, rejected, and discouraged. Because I didn't want people to know what I was going through, I did my best to put on a pleasant face, but deep down, I was hurting badly. During worship, I went and leaned against a pillar—with my face toward the pillar. As we worshipped, I poured my heart to the Lord, and tears flowed down my cheeks. Suddenly, I felt the refreshing presence of the Holy Spirit around me. He wrapped me in His loving arms and said to me, "My son, man did not call you. I called you. I will use you. Look up to me alone and you will see my glory." Hallelujah! With that assurance from the Lord, I felt new strength and energy in my spirit and body. From that day, I cared very little about what anyone thought about my calling because I know I have God's approval.

As our Advocate (Counselor or Attorney), the Holy Spirit speaks in our favor and pleads our cause (John 16:7 NIV). Knowing that we would need this ministry of the Holy Spirit, our Lord Jesus gave us the following assurance:

> When you are brought before synagogues, rulers and authorities, do not worry about how you will defend yourselves or what you will say, for the Holy Spirit will teach you at that time what you should say. (Luke 12:11–12 NIV)

Just as human attorneys stand in court with their clients, the Holy Spirit stands with us through thick and thin, assuring us that we are covered. Like an expert attorney, the Holy Spirit knows and understands all the intricacies of life and stands with us till victory is won. We must, therefore, trust the Holy Spirit to play His advocatory role in our lives by constantly asking Him to lead us and trusting with His infallible counsel. Again, as our Counselor, the Holy Spirit advises, guides, and directs us. Just as we depend on the expertise of professional counselors to guide us in matters such as health, marriage, education, and finance, we must trust the Holy Spirit to counsel, guide, and direct us as well as speak for us.

As a young man in my late twenties, I found myself embroiled in a protracted legal battle. The case was moved from one circuit court to another and then finally to a high court. My adversary never showed up in court, but his attorney presented serious accusations against me that were totally unfounded. To add insult to injury, my attorney connived with my adversary against me and suddenly began to "forget" what he was being paid to do. Sometimes, he "forgot" to file required motions, and other times, he "forgot" to show up in court.

After the case had dragged on for about three years, a Christian brother referred me to another attorney who also happened to be a spirit-filled believer. This new attorney teamed up with me in prayer. We asked the Holy Spirit to intervene. After about three adjournments, the tide suddenly changed. My adversary's attorney stood up in court one day and spoke in my favor. He even apologized for the defense he had previously made, explaining that his client had been feeding him with lies. The Holy Spirit showed up as my advocate-in-chief, and the case was dismissed! Hallelujah! Glory be to God!

## II: The Spirit of Truth

In His pre-Crucifixion discourse with His disciples, Jesus repeatedly assured His disillusioned disciples that He would not leave them helpless. Instead, He would send them (and all who would later believe in Him through the disciples' message) "the Spirit of truth." For example, in John 16:13, Jesus told His disciples:

> When He, the Spirit of truth comes, He will guide you into all the truth. He will not speak on His own; He will speak only what He hears, and He will tell you what is yet to come. (John 16:13 NIV, emphasis mine)

The phrase "He will guide you into all the truth" means the Holy Spirit will lead us or point to us the right or true way. The god of this world (Satan) rules the world system by falsehood and operating through false spirits. As the father of all lies, Satan speaks his native language when he speaks lies. Isn't it refreshing then to know that in an era when satanic agents are pushing for "relative truths," "personal truth" "alternate truth," and "finding one's own truth," God has given us the Spirit of truth?

Deception is and continues to be Satan's most lethal weapon. In the final hours before His Crucifixion, the Lord Jesus Christ gave his disciples the following stern warning against satanic deception:

> Jesus answered: "Watch out that no one deceives you. For many will come in my name, claiming, 'I am the Messiah,' and will deceive many." (Matt 24:4–5 NIV)

Also, in John 14:17, Jesus said to his discouraged disciples:

> And I will ask the Father, and he will give you another advocate to help you and be with you forever—the Spirit of truth. The world cannot accept him, because it neither sees him nor knows him. But you know him, for he lives with you and will be in you. (NIV, emphasis mine)

Again, in John 15:26, Jesus referred to the Holy Spirit as the Spirit of truth.

> When *the Advocate* comes, whom I will send to you from the Father—*the Spirit of truth* who goes out from the Father—He will testify about me. (John 15:26 NIV, emphasis mine)

The expression "Spirit of truth" means that the Holy Spirit is the very embodiment of truth. There is absolutely no error in Him. We can, therefore, trust the Holy Spirit to lead us into all truth. It is also important to point out that every operation of the Holy Spirit is consistent with the totality of God's Word (Logos), which is truth.

## III: Eternal Spirit

This name signifies that the Holy Spirit has no beginning and no ending (Heb. 9:14). It signifies the timeless nature of the Holy Spirit. As the third person of the Holy Trinity, the Holy Spirit's existence, operations, and functions transcend time. He existed before time began and will continue to live when time is no more. The Holy Spirit lives forever. As the eternal Spirit, He sees the past, present, and future simultaneously. If we commit our ways to Him, the Holy Spirit will lead us safely to our God-ordained destiny and will empower us to fulfill our God-ordained purpose during our brief existence on earth.

## IV: The Sevenfold Spirit

In the great Messianic prophesy in Isaiah chapter 11 verse 2, the Bible describes seven distinct characteristics of the Holy Spirit that distinguish the Messiah from everyone else.

> The Spirit of the LORD will rest on him— the Spirit of wisdom and of understanding, the Spirit of counsel and of might, the Spirit of the knowledge and fear of the LORD—[3] and he will delight in the fear of the LORD (NIV).

Since seven signifies completeness and perfection, the Messiah would have the fullness of the Holy Spirit perpetually resting on Him. The sevenfold titles of the Holy Spirit mentioned in Isaiah 11:2 are:

## The Spirit of the LORD

This title affirms that the Holy Spirit is God's Spirit and that He comes from God and has the characteristics of God.

## The Spirit of Wisdom

This means the Holy Spirit gives extraordinary wisdom. Because of the Spirit of wisdom that rested on Joshua, his followers obeyed him (Deut. 34:9). The Holy Spirit-inspired wisdom is "pure, peace-loving, considerate, submissive, full of mercy and good fruit, impartial, and sincere" (James 3:17 NIV). With the Holy Spirit living in us, we have the potential to exercise this "wisdom from above." This gift is yours for the asking, especially if you are serving in a leadership role.

## The Spirit of Understanding

The Holy Spirit gives us a clear sense and comprehension of the purposes of God, the times we are living in, and how we ought to conduct ourselves as God's children (Eph. 5:16). As the source of all divine understanding, the Holy Spirit's job is to help believers make the most of the precious time God gives us, make maximum use of every opportunity God brings us, and thus live wisely. We are told in Job 32:8 that the breath of the Almighty gives us understanding. God's thoughts are infinitely higher than ours. Since there is an immeasurable gap between God's thoughts and our thoughts (Isa. 55:8–9), He gives us His Spirit of understanding to enable us to receive the mind of God (1 Cor. 2:16).

## The Spirit of Counsel

The Holy Spirit is the believer's personal attorney, spokesperson, and knowledgeable guide. He pleads our case and cheers us on till we succeed. He also helps us make the right decisions when faced with challenging issues. All we have to do is to ask Him for His indispensable counsel. Whenever I am faced with difficult situations, I quietly ask the Holy Spirit to intervene. Sometimes He chooses to intervene all by Himself, while in other times, He partners with me to make the right decision.

## The Spirit of Might

The Holy Spirit gives us courage to stand up for what pleases God and the fortitude to withstand negative reactions from those who oppose God and His kingdom. With the Spirit of might living in them, Christians in every century have had to endure unimaginable persecution, suppression, and even death for the sake of their faith. The verdict is clear: the Christian faith cannot be chained even if Christians are chained, and the Christian faith cannot be destroyed even if the faithful are martyred. Why? Because the Spirit of might reigns as Lord of His church!

If you are facing hardships for Christ's sake, please be encouraged. You are in good company. You are sharing in the sufferings of Christ, the Spirit of glory rests on you, and you shall receive the Lord's commendation when He returns (1 Pet. 4:13–14). Moreover, other Christians all over the world are experiencing the same kind of sufferings (1 Pet. 5:9).

## The Spirit of Knowledge

One of the most amazing gifts a believer may receive from the Holy Spirit is the supernatural ability to know things and events that the believer could not know in any other way. Being all-knowing, the Holy Spirit can open the eyes of the understanding of the believer to receive knowledge of future events. Usually, impartation of supernatural knowledge is redemptive in nature. In other occasions, the Holy Spirit gives us such knowledge to confirm something He has already spoken to the individual or church about.

## The Spirit of the Fear of the LORD

The Holy Spirit gives the yielded believer a special revelation of God, which creates in the believer a deep reverence for God. The fear of God draws us into intimate relationship with God. It abhors evil and delights being in the presence of God and in the company of other believers.

## V: The Spirit of Life

This title means that the Holy Spirit is the source of life. It also means the Holy Spirit gives us life. In Romans 8:2, the Bible says, in Christ, the Spirit who gives us life, has set us free from the law of sin and death. Again, in Revelation 11:11 and Ezekiel 37:10, the Holy Spirit is called the Spirit (breath) of life, who causes dead bodies to come back to life.

Romans 8:11 tells us that the same Holy Spirit who raised Jesus from the dead gives life to our mortal bodies because He lives in us. In Ezekiel 37:14, God says "I shall put my Spirit in you and you shall live" (ESV). It is clear from all these passages of scripture that the Holy Spirit is the giver of life.

## VI: The Spirit of Grace and Supplication

This title speaks to the intercessory role the Holy Spirit plays among God's two covenanted people: Israel and the Church. With respect to Israel, God promises to restore them back to their own land, revive them spiritually, and then prosper them economically all through the instrumentality of the Holy Spirit (Ezek. 36:24–31). To the Church, God promises to pour out His Spirit on all flesh, that is people from all backgrounds and status in life (Joel 2:28–29). Out of weaklings, God would raise a strong people for Himself.

> In that day shall the LORD defend the inhabitants of Jerusalem; and he that is feeble among them at that day shall be as David; and the house of David shall be as God, as the angel of the LORD before them. And I will pour upon the house of David, and upon the inhabitants of Jerusalem, the *spirit of grace and of supplications*: and they shall look

upon me whom they have pierced, and they shall mourn for him, as one mourneth for his only son, and shall be in bitterness for him, as one that is in bitterness for his firstborn. (Zechariah 12:8, 10 KJV, emphasis mine)

In response to this restorative act of God, God expects His people to enter into intense intercessory prayer with fasting and to cry out to Him for the *full fulfillment* of His promise (Ezek. 36:37; Joel 1:14; 2:15–17). The Spirit of grace and supplication is being poured on God's covenanted people. Having returned to their own land, Israel is beginning to experience a spiritual revival and economic prosperity. Indeed, a day is coming when the nation of Israel will acknowledge Jesus of Nazareth as their Messiah, and they will wail uncontrollably for crucifying their Lord (v. 10b). In response to their repentance, God will pour out His Spirit on restored Israel (Ezek. 36:26–27).

> **Remember**
>
> *It takes special grace to travail in prayer and it takes intense, sustained supplication to bring down the rain of the Holy Spirit.*

With respect to the Church, the Lord is pouring the Spirit of grace and intercession on millions of His people all over the world for the end-time harvest of souls. Why grace and intercession? It takes special grace to travail in prayer, and it takes intense, sustained supplication to bring down the rain of the Holy Spirit.

> Ask ye of the LORD rain in the time of the latter rain; so the LORD shall make bright clouds, and give them showers of rain, to everyone grass in the field. (Zechariah 10:1 KJV)

It takes the outpouring of the Holy Spirit to bring in the promised end-time harvest of souls. As the Church unites in earnest

*The Holy Spirit*

intercessory prayer for the former and latter rain together, she will experience a supernatural outpouring of God's Spirit the likes of which she has never experienced before.

> Be glad then, ye children of Zion, and rejoice in the LORD your God: for He hath given you the former rain moderately, and *He will cause to come down for you the rain, the former rain, and the latter rain in the first month*.
>
> And the floors shall be *full* of wheat, and the vats shall *overflow* with wine and oil.
>
> And *I will restore* to you the years that the locust hath eaten, the cankerworm, and the caterpillar, and the palmerworm, my great army which I sent among you.
>
> And *ye shall eat in plenty, and be satisfied*, and praise the name of the LORD your God that hath dealt wondrously with you: and my people shall never be ashamed.
>
> And ye shall know that I am in the midst of Israel and that I am the LORD your God, and none else: and my people shall never be ashamed.
>
> And it shall come to pass afterward, that I will pour

---

**Remember**

*It takes the outpouring of the Holy Spirit to bring in the promised end-time harvest of souls.*

---

**Remember**

*As the Church unites in earnest intercessory prayer for the former and latter rain together, she will experience a supernatural outpouring of God's Spirit the likes of which she has never experienced before.*

> out my spirit upon all flesh; and your sons and
> your daughters shall prophesy, your old men shall
> dream dreams, your young men shall see visions:
> And also upon the servants and upon the
> handmaids in those days will I pour out my spirit.
> (Joel 2:23–29 KJV emphasis mine)

Will you respond to God's command to intercede and ask for the rain of the Holy Spirit? God is pouring His Spirit of grace and supplication on His *willing* servants. God is seeking troops who will be willing when the battle lines are drawn. His eyes are moving to and fro over the entire world for people who will offer themselves freely on *this* day of God's power. The LORD is looking for *young people* whose strength He will renew each day.

> Thy people shall be willing in the day of thy power,
> in the beauties of holiness from the womb of the
> morning: thou hast the dew of thy youth. (Ps. 110:3
> KJV, emphasis mine)

> Your troops will be willing on your day of battle.
> Arrayed in holy splendor, your young men will
> come to you like dew from the morning's womb.
> (Ps. 110:3 NIV, emphasis mine)

> For the eyes of the LORD run to and fro throughout
> the whole earth, to shew himself strong in the
> behalf of them whose heart is perfect toward him.
> (2 Chron. 16:9 KJV)

The expression your young men will come to you like dew from the morning's womb signifies strength. God is raising troops of bold, Holy Spirit-filled young people who will defy all odds and champion the cause of Christ and head for the end-time harvest. Just as the dew appears each morning shining on the grass, the strength of these young people God is raising will not wane. They will go from strength to strength. They will be unstoppable. Fully equipped with holy splendor (holy lifestyle), these young warriors will shut the mouth of every would-be accuser. The question once again is: Will you be part of what God is doing in these exciting times?

> *Remember*
>
> *God is raising troops of bold, Holy Spirit-filled young people who will defy all odds and champion the cause of Christ and head for the end-time harvest.*

### VII: The Spirit of Self-Discipline

In 1 Timothy 1:7, the Holy Spirit is described as the one who gives us self-discipline: "For the Spirit God gave us does not make us timid, but gives us power, love and self-discipline" (NIV). The Holy Spirit living inside of us gives us the ability to control ourselves, including our emotions, thoughts, and actions. He helps us to control even our tongues—the part of our bodies the Bible describes as untamable by human willpower. The self-discipline the Holy Spirit gives us also helps us follow through with God's will for our lives when other believers don't understand us. For example, persuaded by the Holy Spirit to go to Rome (even though troubles and imprisonment awaited him), the apostle Paul withstood the dissuasion of the Ephesian church leaders and pursued God's purpose for his life.

> And now, *compelled by the Spirit*, I am going to Jerusalem, not knowing what will happen to me there. I only know that in every city *the Holy Spirit warns me that prison and hardships are facing me.* However, I consider my life worth nothing to me; *my only aim is to finish the race and complete the task the Lord Jesus has given me*—the task of testifying to the good news of God's grace. (Acts 20:22–24 NIV, emphasis mine)

> When we heard this, we and the people there *pleaded with Paul not to go* up to Jerusalem. Then Paul answered, *"Why are you weeping and breaking my heart?* I am ready not only to be bound, but also to die in Jerusalem for the name of the Lord Jesus." *When he would not be dissuaded,* we gave up and said, "The Lord's will be done." (Acts 21:12–13 NIV, emphasis mine)

Any person of lesser self-discipline would have given in to the pleadings of the brethren and would have missed God's revealed will for his life—but not so Paul. His response was:

> But *none of these things move me*, neither count I my life dear unto myself, *so that I might finish my course with joy, and the ministry, which I have received of the Lord Jesus,* to testify the gospel of the grace of God. (Acts 20:24 KJV, emphasis mine)

Paul took seriously the words of the Lord Jesus: "Whoever wants to be my disciple must deny themselves and take up their cross and follow me" (Matt. 16:24 NIV). I believe Paul also remembered the prophetic word he received through Ananias that he (Paul) was a chosen vessel and would experience much suffering for the Lord's sake (Acts 9:15–16). Paul allowed the Holy Spirit to work self-discipline in his life through the things he suffered for the Lord's sake.

> Five times I received from the Jews the forty lashes minus one. Three times I was beaten with rods, once I was pelted with stones, three times I was shipwrecked, I spent a night and a day in the open sea, I have been constantly on the move. I have been in danger from rivers, in danger from bandits, in danger from my fellow Jews, in danger

from Gentiles; in danger in the city, in danger in the country, in danger at sea; and in danger from false believers. I have labored and toiled and have often gone without sleep; I have known hunger and thirst and have often gone without food; I have been cold and naked. Besides everything else, I face daily the pressure of my concern for all the churches. (2 Cor. 11:24–28 KJV)

It is worthy of note that some versions of the Bible translate self-discipline (in 2 Tim. 1:7) as sound mind or sound judgment. I believe this is because it takes self-discipline to make sound judgment, and the self-controlled person has sound mind. The same Spirit who gives us self-discipline also gives us love (agapēs) and power (dunameōs; Acts 1:8). Through the Holy Spirit, God has shed His love abroad in our hearts (Rom. 5:5).

The Holy Spirit has set us free from the slavery of fear and has adopted us as His own sons (mature children), giving us the right to call God "Abba, Father" (Rom. 8:15). It was the Holy Spirit who empowered Stephen to perform great wonders and signs among the people (Acts 6:8) and anointed our Lord Jesus with power as He went about "doing good and healing all who were under the power of the devil" (Acts 10:38 NIV). In a nutshell, the Holy Spirit is indispensable for living a fruitful life.

## Divine Attributes

Divine attributes are the characteristics that distinguish God from all other beings. The major distinctive attributes of God are eternity, omnipresence, omniscience, and omnipotence. As the third person of the Trinity, the Holy Spirit demonstrates all four distinctive divine characteristics in scripture and in our daily lives. We shall examine some of these divine characteristics from scripture.

## I: Eternity

Scripture tells us the Holy Spirit is eternal. In the fourth verse of Hebrews chapter nine, we read:

> How much more, then, will the blood of Christ, who through the eternal Spirit offered himself unblemished to God, cleanse our consciences from acts that lead to death, so that we may serve the living God! (Heb. 9:4 NIV)

In the scripture above, the Bible describes the Holy Spirit as eternal. That means the Holy Spirit has always existed and will continue to exist forever. He has no beginning and no ending. As the third person of the Holy Trinity, the Holy Spirit is self-existent. The fact that the Holy Spirit is eternal should give you comfort because He has your past, present, and future all covered. He knows the way ahead of you and offers you a great future if you allow Him to direct every step of your life. When you trust Him completely with your life, He will uphold, guide, and empower you to do exploits beyond your wildest imagination. He is your indispensable helper for eternity!

> *Remember*
>
> *The Holy Spirit knows the way ahead of you and offers you a great future if you allow Him to direct every step of your life.*

## II: Omnipresence

Omnipresence is the distinguishing characteristic of God that makes Him capable of filling all space and pervading all things with His invisible and immaterial substance.

*The Holy Spirit*

> "Am I only a God nearby," declares the LORD, "and not a God far away? "Who can hide in secret places so that I cannot see them?" declares the LORD. "Do not I fill heaven and earth?" declares the LORD. (Jer. 23:23–24 NIV)

Omnipresence is an exclusive attribute of God. Only God is capable of being everywhere at the same time. The Holy Spirit is omnipresent because He is everywhere at the same time.

> Where can I go from your Spirit? Where can I flee from your presence? If I go up to the heavens, you are there; if I make my bed in the depths, you are there. If I rise on the wings of the dawn, if I settle on the far side of the sea, even there your hand will guide me, your right hand will hold me fast. (Ps. 139:7–10 NIV)

Trying to hide from God the Holy Spirit is an act in futility because He is everywhere. He literally fills the entire universe—both visible and invisible. Unlike us, the Holy Spirit is not limited by space and time. The Holy Spirit's omnipresence enables Him to make special manifestations to different people at various locations at the same time. For example, the Holy Spirit is manifesting His awesome healing power and saving grace in many different meetings in different countries right now. He is filing and blessing hundreds of thousands of God's people all over the world as you read this book. The lives of thousands of people all over the world are being turned around for good by the infinite mercy and grace of the Holy Spirit. All these manifestations show that the Holy Spirit is omnipresent.

> **Remember**
>
> *The Holy Spirit is an infinite observer of every single thing we do no matter where and when we do it.*

No one can escape the presence of the Holy Spirit. He is in all places at all times! He is present wherever we go. No place is too far or too obscure or too dark for the Holy Spirit to be present. In a sense, the Holy Spirit is an infinite observer of every single thing we do—no matter where and when we do it. He is present with us when we are in an open space like a field or in a private place such as a bedroom. His presence is with us in busy places like an assembly plant, in a commercial place like a shopping mall, and in places of suffering and pain like the hospital. No matter where you are and no matter your circumstances, the Holy Spirit is there to comfort, strengthen, guide, heal, and meet your present need.

If you find it difficult to wrap your mind around this truth, it is because it is impossible to fathom this divine attribute called omnipresence with the finite mind. The comforting aspect of this truth, however, is that the Holy Spirit is ever-present with us not to condemn us but to guide and support us and hold us fast with His right hand (Ps. 139:10 NIV). The Holy Spirit's divine attribute of omnipresence is another reason why He is our indispensable Helper!

### III: Omniscience

Omniscience simply means the capacity (of a being) to know everything. The Bible is clear that the Holy Spirit has infinite knowledge and understanding. There is nothing the Holy Spirit does not know. Nothing is hidden from Him. The omniscience of the Holy Spirit goes hand-in-hand with His omnipresence. He is everywhere and knows everything. Psalm 139 captures this truth in the most magnificent way:

> Where can I go from your Spirit? Where can I flee from your presence? If I go up to the heavens, you are there; if I make my bed in the depths, you are there. If I rise on the wings of the dawn, if I settle on the far side of the sea, even there your hand will

guide me, your right hand will hold me fast. If I say, "Surely the darkness will hide me and the light become night around me," even the darkness will not be dark to you; the night will shine like the day, for darkness is as light to you (Ps. 139:7–13 NIV).

The prophet Isaiah expressed similar sentiments when he stood in amazement of the awesome knowledge and understanding of the Spirit of God:

> Who can fathom the Spirit of the LORD, or instruct the LORD as his counselor? Whom did the LORD consult to enlighten him, and who taught him the right way? Who was it that taught him knowledge, or showed him the path of understanding? (Isa. 40:13,14 NIV)

Only the Holy Spirit knows it all. Therefore, we can confidently ask Him to instruct and counsel us. In Him, we find an inexhaustible treasure trove of knowledge, understanding, and insight. The good news is He is eager to unleash and lavish these treasures on us. The question is, Are you willing to ask Him for them?

## IV: Omnipotence

The term omnipotence means unlimited or infinite power. Omnipotence is one of the four distinctive attributes of God. Though some of God's creations—the sun, the oceans, and kings—have delegated with varied forms of power, only God is all-powerful. Power belongs to God (Ps. 62:11). This is why He is called Almighty God, the Most High God. God's omnipotence is best captured by His name YHWH "I Am That I Am," meaning the self-existent, unchanging One who does what He likes, how He likes it, and no one has the right to question Him. God's power is incomparable. Here are few scriptures that highlight God's omnipotence.

> Behold, I am the LORD, the God of all flesh: is there *anything* too hard for me? (Jer. 32:27 KJV)

After his seven years of humiliation for not acknowledging God's sovereignty, Nebuchadnezzar praised the Most High; he honored and glorified Him who lives forever with the following words:

> All the peoples of the earth are regarded as nothing. *He (God) does as he pleases* with the *powers of heaven* and the peoples of the earth. *No one can hold back his hand or say to him: "What have you done?* (Dan. 4:35 NIV, emphasis mine)

> Human beings are beset with many impossible situations, but *with God all things are possible.* (Matt. 19:26 NIV, emphasis mine)

Job said it best when he said this of the LORD:

> I know that *you can do all things*; no purpose of yours can be thwarted. (Job 42:1–2 NIV, emphasis mine)

All three persons of the Trinity exercise the distinctive divine attribute of omnipotence. For example, during creation, the Father demonstrated His omnipotence by speaking the universe into existence and sustaining it by the Word of His power.

> Through Him (the Son) all things were made; without Him, nothing was made that has been made. (John 1:3 NIV)

Moreover, in the Son, "all things hold together" (Col. 1:17 NIV). By the Spirit of the Lord, the entire universe was made (Job 26:13; Gen. 1:1–3).

Another evidence of the omnipotence of the Holy Spirit is in how He overshadowed the Virgin Mary to conceive the Lord Jesus. When angel Gabriel announced to Mary that she was going to be the mother of the promised Messiah, she asked the angel, "How will this be, since I am a virgin?"

The angel answered, "The Holy Spirit will come on you, and the power of the Most High will overshadow you. So, the holy one to be born will be called the Son of God" (Luke 1:34–35 NIV).

To further assure Mary that the Holy Spirit could do anything, Gabriel told Mary that her cousin, Elizabeth, who people ridiculed for being barren, was six months pregnant. It takes an omnipotent person to cause a virgin and a barren woman to become pregnant.

A third evidence of the omnipotence of the Holy Spirit is in resurrecting the Lord Jesus Christ from the dead (Rom. 11:2). The assurance is that since the same Spirit who raised Jesus from death lives in us, He will quicken our mortal bodies.

A fourth evidence of the omnipotence of the Holy Spirit is that He imparts power to millions of believers. Jesus's promise, "You will receive power when the Holy Spirit comes on you" (Acts 1:8), was fulfilled on the day of Pentecost and continues till now. The power of the Holy Spirit must be infinite to pour out on millions of people without running out.

## Divine Works Attributed to the Holy Spirit

There are three works that are distinctively attributed to God: creation, impartation of life, and the origination of the Holy Scriptures. All these three divine works are accredited to the Holy Spirit.

### I: Creation

The Bible ascribes creation of the universe to the Holy Spirit in partnership with the Father and the Son:

> In the beginning, God created the heavens and the earth. Now the earth was formless and, darkness was over the surface of the deep, and *the Spirit of God was hovering over the waters*. And God said, "Let there be light," and there was light. (Gen. 1:1–3 NIV, emphasis mine)

In his commentary of the wonder of creation, the Psalmist soliloquized:

> You (Father God) created all of them *by your Spirit*, and you give new life to the earth. (Ps. 104:30 CEV, emphasis mine)

The indispensable role of the Holy Spirit in creation was discussed extensively in chapter two.

## II: Impartation of Life

You may recall that one of the names of the Holy Spirit is the Spirit of life, meaning the Holy Spirit has life in Himself and, therefore, *can* impart life to others. In the creation of humans, it was the Spirit (breath) of God that gave life to them (Gen. 2:7). Also, but for the Holy Spirit, Jesus's body would have rotted in the grave. It was the Holy Spirit who imparted life to the dead body of Jesus Christ and thus raised Him (Jesus) from the dead (Rom. 8:11). The same Holy Spirit who raised the Lord Jesus from the dead imparts His life to us (Rom. 8:11). This divine life of the Spirit gives us good health and restores us back to health when we fall sick.

## III: Originator of Scripture

The third distinctive work of God is the authorship of scripture. The Bible makes it unequivocally clear that none of the forty men

*The Holy Spirit*

who wrote the scriptures penned their own ideas or thoughts but all of them were inspired (carried along) by the Holy Spirit.

> Above all, you must understand that no prophecy of scripture came about by the prophet's own interpretation of things. For prophecy never had its origin in the human will, but prophets, though human, spoke from God as they were carried along by the Holy Spirit. (2 Pet. 1:20–21 NIV)

The men God used themselves knew and understood that the words they spoke and wrote were indeed the Word of God as evidenced by what they wrote:

- Ezekiel: *The Word of the LORD came unto me* again, saying … (Ezekiel 18:1 KJV, emphasis mine)
- Zechariah: Moreover *the word of the LORD came unto me*, saying … (Zech. 4:8 KJV, emphasis mine)
- David: *The Spirit of the LORD spoke through me*; His word was on my tongue. (2 Sam. 23:2 NIV, emphasis mine)
- Jeremiah: *The Word of the LORD came to me*, saying, "Before I formed you in the womb I knew you, before you were born I set you apart; I appointed you as a prophet to the nations." (Jer. 1:4–5 NIV, emphasis mine)

Everything they wrote was inspired (God-breathed) by the Holy Spirit. In other words, the Holy Spirit ensured that only God's Word was written and not the thoughts of the human instruments. Thus, the real author of scripture is the Holy Spirit. This is why we can confidently accept the scriptures (in its entirety and in all its parts) as the infallible, inerrant Word of God.

> *All Scripture is given by inspiration of God*, and *is* profitable for doctrine, for reproof, for correction,

for instruction in righteousness. (2 Tim. 3:16 NKJV, emphasis mine)

It can't be overemphasized: all scripture is inspired by God. The prophets who penned the scriptures wrote only what the Spirit of God inspired them to write (2 Pet. 1:19–21). Therefore, if we need accurate interpretation of any part of scripture, the best person to ask is the author—the Holy Spirit.

## The Symbols of the Holy Spirit

The Bible often uses symbolic language to describe people and situations. These symbols describe the distinctive nature and/or functions of the person or thing being symbolized. For example, in a prophetic prelude to the Holy Spirit-empowered ministry of the Messiah, the prophet Isaiah describes the Messiah as a "shoot from the stem of Jesse" and a "branch" springing "from his roots" (11:1 NASB), meaning the Messiah would be a descendant of Jesse.

In the same vein, various symbols are used to describe the Holy Spirit in the Bible. These symbols do not in any way mean the Holy Spirit is an impersonal entity. He is a Person. However, He chooses to manifest Himself in various symbols to demonstrate to us an aspect of His ministry or personality.

It is the prerogative of the Holy Spirit to decide how and when to manifest Himself to whoever He chooses to manifest Himself. We cannot determine how we want the Holy Spirit to manifest Himself. For example, I have had the rare privilege of seeing the Holy Spirit manifest Himself in the glory cloud on two separate occasions, but on both occasions, we had no idea He was going to show up in that fashion. On both occasions, the Holy Spirit manifested His presence in the meetings as a gentle, white smoke. In the first instance, the glory cloud rolled slowly from the back of the auditorium, and as it did so, the congregation gently fell under the power when the glory cloud got to where they were standing.

However, in the second instance, the glory cloud rolled from the front seat, and everyone who encountered the manifest presence of the Holy Spirit was slain in the Spirit—row by row. It was an awesome sight, and the atmosphere was reverential.

When Elijah requested to see the glory of God, he expected to find God in the wind, earthquake, and fire, but God chose to speak to him in a still small voice (1 Kings 19:11–13). We don't get to decide how the Holy Spirit should manifest Himself to us. He does. He may decide to manifest Himself in the form of one symbol or another. Sometimes He manifests Himself in spectacular forms as a glory cloud as I and many others saw in those meetings, or He may choose to give us a quiet inner affirmation in our hearts, assuring us, "I'm here. You're good."

I will now discuss some of the symbols used in the Bible to describe the Holy Spirit. As you prayerfully reflect on these symbols, I pray that the Holy Spirit will open the eyes of your understanding to comprehend the depth of God's love for you.

**I: Rain**

The Holy Spirit is often depicted in scripture as rain. As rain, the presence of the Holy Spirit causes all spiritual dryness in our lives to give way to a refreshing, new life of abundance and prosperity. For example, in Joel chapter 2, there is a double prophecy of natural rain resulting in abundant harvest and outpouring of spiritual rain of the Holy Spirit resulting in spiritual awakening and revival.

> Be glad then, you children of Zion, And rejoice in the LORD your God; For He has given you the former rain faithfully, And He will cause the rain to come down for you—*The former rain, and the latter rain in the first month.* The threshing floors shall be full of wheat, And the vats shall overflow with new wine and oil. (Joel 2:23–24 NKJV, emphasis mine)

Rain also symbolizes divine provisions, taking away of past reproach, and restoration of lost blessings:

> So I will *restore to you the years* that the swarming locust has eaten, the crawling locust, the consuming locust, and the chewing locust, My great army which I sent among you. *You shall eat in plenty and be satisfied*, and praise the name of the Lord your God, Who has dealt wondrously with you; and *My people shall never be put to shame*. Then you shall know that I am in the midst of Israel: I am the LORD your God and there is no other. *My people shall never be put to shame.* (Joel 2:25–27 NKJV, emphasis mine)

Moreover, rain is a type of the outpouring of the Holy Spirit, resulting in ordinary people everywhere exercising supernatural abilities (such as prophesying and seeing of visions and dreams), which were the means by which God communicated to and through Old Testament prophets and sometimes kings:

> And it shall come to pass afterward *That I will pour out My Spirit* on all flesh; Your sons and your daughters *shall prophesy*, Your old men *shall dream dreams*, Your young men *shall see visions*. And also on My menservants and on My maidservants I will pour out My Spirit in those days. (Joel 2:28–29 NKJV, emphasis mine)

This wonderful rain of the Holy Spirit was first poured out on the day of Pentecost. On that day, the seeds of the Gospel were sowed, and three thousand souls were added to the church. That was the early rain. The latter rain has been falling since the turn of the last century, resulting in mighty outpourings of the Holy Spirit on the church all over the world. As the end-time draws to a close, the

LORD is pouring on His people the former rain and the latter rain together (Joel 2:23). This double rain, which is meant to usher in the end-time harvest of souls into God's kingdom, is falling and available to as many as are thirsty for the Holy Spirit.

It is worthy of note that just as rain is given, in the natural, for the purpose of a harvest, the rain of the Holy Spirit is given primarily for the great harvest of souls into the kingdom of God. God expects us to be drenched in the rain of the Holy Spirit for the end-time harvest of souls into His kingdom.

## II: Rivers

The Holy Spirit is also typified in scriptures as rivers. He is portrayed as the source of adequate supply for humanity's innermost need. He comes to refresh and completely fill dry, thirsty human vessels and make them His channels of blessings to other spiritually thirsty people. Jesus underscored this truth:

> On the last day, that great day of the feast, Jesus stood and cried out, saying, "If anyone thirsts, let him come to Me and drink. He who believes in Me, as the Scripture has said, *out of his heart will flow rivers of living water.*" But this He spoke concerning *the Spirit*, whom those *believing in Him would receive*; for the Holy Spirit was not yet given, because Jesus was not yet glorified. (John 7:37–39 NIV, emphasis mine)

The amazing thing about what Jesus is saying here is that the Holy Spirit (as symbolized by rivers of living water) transforms a thirsty person into an overflowing tributary! When the rivers of the Holy Spirit fill you, you will be refreshed, and you become a conduit and an extension of God's blessings to the spiritually needy people you meet. The Holy Spirit flows out of your life like an ever-fresh stream of living water that refreshes the people you encounter.

Thus, receiving the Holy Spirit to overflow is not only for your own benefit; it is also for the good of others.

## III: Wind

When Bible speaks of the Holy Spirit as wind, it depicts His awesome power. Speaking with Nicodemus about the new birth experience, Jesus indicated that though the Holy Spirit is invisible, He is powerful enough to bring about inner transformation. Jesus told Nicodemus that:

> The wind blows where it wishes, and you hear the sound of it, but cannot tell where it comes from and where it goes. So is everyone who is born of the Spirit. (John 3:8 ESV)

The irresistible power of the Holy Spirit was amply displayed at the outset of the Church:

> When the Day of Pentecost had fully come, they were all with one accord in one place. And suddenly there came a sound from heaven, as of *a rushing mighty wind,* and it filled the whole house where they were sitting. Then there appeared to them divided tongues, as of fire, and one sat upon each of them. And *they were all filled with the Holy Spirit* and began to speak with other tongues, as the Spirit gave them utterance. (Acts 2:1–3 NKJV, emphasis mine)

The same mighty rushing wind (of the Holy Spirit) that filled the house also filled the disciples. That sound of the heavenly wind, coupled with the speaking in other tongues, attracted bystanders to see what the Lord was doing in the midst of His people. The wind of the Holy Spirit is still blowing all over the world, convicting sinners, causing rebirth, and filling saints for greater works. Furthermore, since the Hebrew and Greek words for wind may also be translated as breath, wind symbolizes the life-giving breath of the Holy Spirit on the church.

## IV: Oil

Oil symbolizes anointing for supernatural ministry. Believers in Christ have received "an anointing from the Holy One" (1 John 2:20, 27). This anointing sets us apart from the world unto God's service and teaches us the truth. Just as the Old Testament prophets, priest, and kings were anointed with oil (symbolizing the Holy Spirit), believers in Christ have also received a special anointing to play our prophetic, priestly, and kingly roles.

As New Testament prophets, Christians are anointed with the Holy Spirit to be God's spokespeople. As Christ's ambassadors, God makes His appeal through us (2 Cor. 5:20). Similarly, as New Testament priests, the Holy Spirit anoints us to offer up spiritual sacrifices comprising worship and intercessions:

> You also, like living stones, are being built into a spiritual house to be a *holy priesthood, offering spiritual sacrifices* acceptable to God through Jesus Christ. (1 Pet. 2:5 NIV, emphasis mine)

> Through Jesus, therefore, let us continually offer to God a sacrifice of praise—the fruit of lips that openly profess his name (Heb. 13:15 NIV)

Moreover, as New Testament kings, the Holy Spirit anoints us to exercise kingdom dominion and authority on earth, especially in our homes, businesses, and ministries. Whatever we allow on earth will be permitted in heaven, and whatever we forbid on earth will be forbidden in heaven (Matt. 18:18).

The oil of the Holy Spirit upon us is also a seal of ownership signifying that we are God's possession forever:

> Now it is God who makes both us and you stand firm in Christ. *He anointed us, set his seal of ownership on us, and put His Spirit in our hearts* as a deposit, guaranteeing what is to come. (2 Cor. 1:21–22 NIV)

Think about it. The presence (anointing) of the Holy Spirit in our lives is God's deposit or down payment guaranteeing our redemptive inheritance. That is a staggering thought! The anointing of the Holy Spirit on believers is God's pledge or "deposit guaranteeing our inheritance until the redemption of those who are God's possession—to the praise of His glory" (Eph. 1:14 NASB). The oil of the Holy Spirit upon our lives signifies God's seal of approval, which was also on Jesus (John 6:27). Astonished by the weight of God's goodness to us in Christ, Paul launch into a doxology "to the praise of His glory" (Eph. 1:14 NIV).

**V: Wine**

When the Holy Spirit is symbolized as wine, it speaks of the influence He exerts on us when we willingly submit the control of our lives to Him. The Holy Spirit, as the new wine, must be placed in new wineskin; that is the regenerated person (Mark 2:22). When such a life allows the new wine of the Spirit to stretch, it produces the kind of result the wine breeder intended it to produce. In Ephesians 5:18, the Bible compares the person who is controlled by the Holy Spirit to the one controlled by wine:

> And don't get drunk with wine, which leads to reckless actions, but be filled by the Spirit. (Eph. 5:18 Holman Christian Standard Bible)

When a person is under the control of natural wine, their actions are reckless, but when they are led or controlled or filled with the wine of the Holy Spirit, they experience order in their actions. This is why Christians are commanded to "let the Holy Spirit guide your lives. Then you won't be doing what your sinful nature craves" (Gal. 5:16 NIV).

When you yield your will fully to the Holy Spirit, you will bear the fruit of the Spirit, which is "love, joy, peace, forbearance, kindness, goodness, faithfulness, gentleness and self-control" (Gal. 5:22–23 NIV). Our responsibility is to *yield control of our lives* to the Holy Spirit—all the time. God wants us to be filled with (controlled by) the new wine of the Holy Spirit consistently and continuously. That is how we can experience victory in our lives. We have a part to play as much as God has His part.

## VI: Fire

The Holy Spirit is symbolized as fire. On the day of Pentecost, the Holy Spirit manifested Himself in the form of flames or tongues of fire.

> Then, what looked like *flames or tongues of fire* appeared and settled on each of them. And everyone present was *filled with the Holy Spirit* and began to speak in other languages as the Holy Spirit gave them utterance. (Acts 2:3–4 NLT, emphasis mine)

Fire signifies purification and consecration. Just as fire refines silver and other precious metals, the Holy Spirit fire purifies and refines us and sets us apart for the Lord's holy use. The Spirit of fire cleanses and washes us from all our filth and sin stains (Isa. 4:4). No matter how sin-stained you are, the Lord is willing to wash and cleanse you right now by the fire of the Holy Spirit. He will dump your sins in the sea of forgetfulness (Mic. 7:19) and consecrate you for His holy use (2 Tim. 2:21). If you need cleansing and consecration, please close the book for a minute and get right with God.

## VII: Dove

This is, by far, the most widely known symbol of the Holy Spirit. The symbolism of the dove depicts the gentleness and peace the Holy Spirit bestows. After His water baptism, the Holy Spirit came upon Jesus as a dove and the Father God spoke from heaven affirming His approval of Jesus as His beloved Son:

> And when Jesus was baptized, immediately he went up from the water, and behold, the heavens were opened to him, and *he saw the Spirit of God descending like a dove* and coming to rest on him; and behold, a voice from heaven said, "This is my beloved Son, with whom I am well pleased." (Matt. 3:16–17 ESV, emphasis mine)

When we allow the Holy Spirit to be the Lord of our lives, He produces gentleness in our lives and releases His peace, which passes all understanding in our lives.

# Chapter 5

## Indispensable in Old Testament Ministry

*All the people that made a difference for God
in their generation did so by the anointing
of the Holy Spirit upon their lives.*

THE EARTH WAS STILL very young when Enoch was born. In fact, Adam was only 622 years old when Enoch was born (Gen. 5:3–18). At a time when the average life expectancy was nine hundred years, Adam was still in his prime when Enoch was born. As a contemporary of Adam, Enoch undoubtedly tapped into Adam's insight about what it took to walk with God. In your mind's eye, can you see Enoch visiting his great grandfather after a hard day's work? As the two men strolled in the beautiful garden belonging to Adam, Enoch would ask his great grandfather Adam how it was like having Almighty God visit with him in the garden and to walk with God. With a sense of nostalgia, Adam would describe to Enoch the ecstasy of having fellowship with God. As he spoke, a deep desire to experience a deeper, more intimate relationship with God would well up in Enoch. Thus, began Enoch's extraordinary experience of walking with God.

Enoch is the first person mentioned in scripture to have walked faithfully with God; the only other person so described is Enoch's great-grandson, Noah (Gen. 6:9). Unlike his ancestors, who lived and died, Enoch had the singular honor of being the first person not to experience death because God whisked him away. The only other person who had this honor was the prophet Elijah (2 Kings 2:11). Everything about Enoch was record shattering. His son, Methuselah, lived 969 years, the longest on earth (Gen. 5:25).

So, who really was Enoch? How did he receive such extraordinary favor with God, and what lessons can we learn from this unsung hero of our faith? We would glean the few scriptures that talk about this incredible man of God in order to learn the secrets of his extraordinary life. Of particular interest would be the indispensable role the Holy Spirit played in Enoch's walk with God.

## Who Was Enoch?

Enoch's name is mentioned only nine times in the entire Bible: six times in Genesis 5:18–24, once in 1 Chronicles 1:3, once in Hebrews 11:5, and once in Jude 14. In the Genesis account, we learn that Enoch was the son of Jared, the great-great-great grandson of Adam and the father of the longest living man, Methuselah. Moreover, Enoch was the great grandfather of Noah.

Though Enoch lived at a time when there was much evil on the face of earth (Gen. 6:5–6), he learned to walk with God after giving birth to his son, Methuselah.

> When Enoch was sixty-five years old, he became the father of Methuselah. Enoch walked [in habitual fellowship] with God three hundred years after the birth of Methuselah and had other sons and daughters. So, all the days of Enoch were three hundred and sixty-five years. And [in reverent fear and obedience] Enoch walked with God; and he was not [found among men], because

God took him [away to be home with Him]. (Gen. 5:21–24 AMP)

## Why Did Enoch Please God?

The book of Hebrews gives us an idea about why God was pleased with Enoch:

> By faith Enoch was taken from this life, so that he did not experience death: "He could not be found, because God had taken him away"; for before he was taken, he was commended as one who pleased God. And without faith it is impossible to please God, because anyone who comes to Him must believe that He exists and that He rewards those who earnestly seek Him. (Hebrews chapter 11:5–NIV)

In Genesis 5:21–24 and Hebrews 11:5–6, we can identify several reasons why Enoch pleased God. He made a decision to have consistent fellowship with God. For three hundred years, Enoch had habitual fellowship with God. He made a habit of meeting with God—consistently. Enoch made a decision to have unbroken fellowship with God, and he kept his word. He literally lived in God's presence 24/7. He had constant communication and communion with God.

Enoch walked by faith. He acknowledged the existence of God and lived to honor God. Though God is Spirit and cannot be seen, Enoch believed God and had tangible fellowship with God. He also believed that God rewards those who diligently seek him.

Also, Enoch chose to walk away from the evil practices of his day and dared to live according to the revealed will of God. That was quite an unpopular thing to do. It was politically incorrect. He rejected the accepted norms of his day that were contrary to God's commands. He was loyal to God. "Do two walk together unless they have agreed to do so?" (Amos 3:3 NIV).

We can infer that Enoch's decision to walk with God was as a result of an agreement he made with God. He sought to worship God unreservedly in spirit and in truth. The closer he walked with God, the farther he got from the world. The more Enoch walked with God, the more the world was unworthy of him. He could not have been God's friend while loving the world at the same time. The Holy Spirit revealed to this Old Testament saint what was later articulated in the New Testament by the Lord's brother, James.

> **Remember**
>
> *The more Enoch walked with God, the more the world was unworthy of him.*

Friendship with the world means enmity against God. Therefore, anyone who chooses to be a friend of the world becomes an enemy of God. (James 4:4 NIV)

When we consider that the people of Enoch's generation were "wicked and every inclination of the thoughts of their hearts were only evil at all time" (Gen. 6:5 NIV), it must have been very courageous on Enoch's part to have walked with God. He understood that walking with God was a life of constant faith in God as well as constant fellowship with God. So, how could Enoch remain righteous and faithful to God in the midst of so much evil that engulfed him? The answer is he had the Holy Spirit as his indispensable Helper and Friend.

> **Remember**
>
> *How could Enoch remain righteous and faithful to God in the midst of so much evil that engulfed him? The answer is he had the Holy Spirit as his indispensable Helper and Friend.*

Enoch, the seventh from Adam, prophesied about them: "See, the Lord is coming with thousands upon thousands of his holy ones to judge everyone, and to convict all of them of all the ungodly acts they have committed in their ungodliness and of all the defiant words ungodly sinners have spoken against him." (Jude 14–15 NIV)

According to Jude, not only did God speak with Enoch, but God also set him aside as His spokesman. In fact, Enoch was a prophet of God, who prophesied about the Second Coming of Jesus Christ. This means that Enoch had the anointing of the Holy Spirit on him because "prophets, though human, spoke from God as they were carried along by the Holy Spirit" (2 Pet. 1:21 NIV).

Enoch also prophesied about God's imminent judgment against his generation. As a prophet, Enoch named his son Methuselah, meaning "When he is dead, it shall be sent." The little word "it" referred to the great flood that took place in Noah's time. Thus, Methuselah was a walking, breathing warning about the coming Flood. His existence on earth was a constant reminder to the people of his generation that God was about to destroy the earth with a flood. The fact that he lived the longest in human history is a testament to the mercy and forbearance of God.

Methuselah fathered Lamech at age 187 (Gen. 5:25), and Lamech fathered Noah when he was 182 years. Noah was 600 years when the Flood came. Thus, Methuselah was (187 + 182 + 600) years = 969 years when the flood came (Gen. 7:11). "Thus all the days of Methuselah were 969 years, and he died" (Gen. 5:2 ESV). Therefore, Methuselah died in the very year of Noah's Flood but possibly before it began just as his prophetic name indicated (Gen. 5:25–29; 7:11). How could Enoch give such an accurate prophecy? The answer, once again, is he had the Holy Spirit as his indispensable Revelator and Friend.

## How Did Enoch Walk with God?

I strongly believe Enoch might have had an encounter with God that totally changed the course of his life. No one ever encounters God and remains the same. It is also my firm conviction that Enoch, at a certain point in his life, made an unwavering decision to reject the luring attractions of the world and live completely for God. That decision, no doubt, might have attracted ridicule from the people around him and must have even cost him the loss of some close friends. Though they may have called him all kinds of derogatory names, Enoch remained steadfast because he depended on his indispensable helper and friend—the Holy Spirit.

Next, Enoch might have spent quality time with God. He understood that any relationship worth its salt must be nurtured through intimate fellowship, open communication, and mutual commitment. As Enoch opened up his life to God, the Holy Spirit revealed mysteries to him. God delighted in Enoch and trusted him so much that He took him away from the earth in the prime of his life.

## What Lessons Can We Learn from Enoch?

- Walking with God requires turning our backs on the trappings of the world system.
- Walking with God must be intentional; it requires a steadfast decision.
- Spending time with God should be our highest priority.
- We must be willing to pay the high price of walking with God.
- When we are in God's presence, we must be willing and ready to:
    - hear from the Holy Spirit
    - lay down our own ambitions and plans
    - follow the directions of our indispensable helper and teacher, the Holy Spirit

## Bezalel

Bezalel (also called Bezaleel in the King James Version of the Bible) had the distinguished honor of being the first man mentioned in scripture as "filled with the Spirit of God." That is not to say he was the first man filled with the Holy Spirit in scripture, but he was the first man of whom scripture explicitly says he was filled with the Holy Spirit. His name is mentioned six times in the Bible: once in Exodus 31:1–2; once in Exodus 35:30–35; twice in Exodus 36:1–2; once in Exodus 37:1; and once in Exodus 38:22. He was the son of Uri, the grandson of Moses's special helper, Hur, and was from the tribe of Judah.

> Then the Lord said to Moses, "See, I have chosen Bezalel son of Uri, the son of Hur, of the tribe of Judah, and I have filled him with the Spirit of God, with wisdom, with understanding, with knowledge and with all kinds of skills—to make artistic designs for work in gold, silver and bronze, to cut and set stones, to work in wood, and to engage in all kinds of crafts." (Exodus 31:1–5 NIV)

The first thing that impresses me in this passage is that when the Lord earmarks a person, He calls him by name and then goes ahead to pinpoint him by lineage. He leaves no doubt about the person He is calling. Second, the Lord revealed to Moses that He had equipped Bezalel with special artistic skills of craftsmanship. The third thing we see in this passage is that Bezalel's extraordinary skills were the result of God filling him with His Spirit. Hallelujah! The Holy Spirit imparted to Bezalel special "wisdom and ability, understanding and intelligence, and knowledge, and all kinds of craftsmanship; the ability to devise skillful works, to work in gold, and in silver, and in bronze; and cutting of stones for setting, and carving of wood" (Exo. 30:3–5 NKJV). Bezalel's calling indicates that God fills people with His

Spirit not only for preaching, teaching, singing, and healing ministries but also for artistry.

Typically, craftsmen specialize in either woodwork, metalwork, or stonework, but in the case of Bezalel, the Holy Spirit gave him special wisdom, knowledge, and skills of craftsmanship in all three specialties. He was an expert in molding and cutting "gold, silver and bronze; in cutting jewels for setting, in carving wood, and to work in all manner of artistic workmanship" (Exo. 35:32–33 NIV). In addition, the Holy Spirit gave him extraordinary skills in crafting textiles. Bezalel received from the Holy Spirit a special ability to visualize the tabernacle and its vessels of worship as described to him by Moses. Together with other exceptionally gifted men such as Oholiab of the tribe of Dan, Bezalel constructed the tabernacle and made all the holy vessels of worship exactly as God had revealed to Moses on the Mountain.

> Moreover, I have appointed Oholiab son of Ahisamak, of the tribe of Dan, to help him. Also I have given ability to all the skilled workers to make everything I have commanded you: the tent of meeting, the ark of the covenant law with the atonement cover on it, and all the other furnishings of the tent—the table and its articles, the pure gold lampstand and all its accessories, the altar of incense, the altar of burnt offering and all its utensils, the basin with its stand—and also the woven garments, both the sacred garments for Aaron the priest and the garments for his sons when they serve as priests, and the anointing oil and fragrant incense for the Holy Place. They are to make them just as I commanded you. (Exo. 31:6–11 NIV)

The Holy Spirit also made Bezalel skillful to do all manner of engraving, designing, and making of tapestry with "blue, purple, and scarlet thread, and fine linen; as well as weaving (Exod. 35:35). As the great Teacher, the Holy Spirit gave Bezalel the ability to teach other craftsmen his divinely imparted skills of craftsmanship. Moreover, the Holy Spirit gave Bezalel special leadership skills to plan, coordinate, and execute this divinely appointed work.

Everybody and everything that is devoted to God's service had to be set apart. Every one of the priests, including Aaron, the high priest, had to be consecrated before attending to the LORD's service (Lev. 8–10; Exo. 29:42–49)). The ceremonial vessels used in the tabernacle were also sanctified for the LORD's use (Num. 7:1). No wonder the LORD deemed it fit to set apart the man who would spearhead the construction of the Tabernacle and make its utensils of worship by filling him with Holy Spirit. Thus, we see the indispensable role of the Holy Spirit demonstrated in the life of Bezalel for craftsmanship.

## Gideon

Gideon was anything but a courageous man. Having experienced seven years of cruel oppression by the Midianites, Gideon, like the rest of Israel, lived in constant fear of their ruthless oppressors. It, therefore, sounded like sarcasm when an angel of the LORD appeared to Gideon on the threshing floor and addressed him as a "mighty man of valor" (Judges 6:12). God, who sees the end from the beginning, was speaking to Gideon about the supernatural transformation that was about to take place in Gideon's life because of His Spirit coming upon Gideon.

"The Spirit of the LORD came upon Gideon; then he blew the trumpet," (Judges 6:34 NIV) and he completely defeated the Midianites with only three hundred divinely appointed men. It was the Spirit of the LORD coming upon Gideon that drastically transformed him from a coward into a mighty military leader. Step-by-step, Gideon followed God's strategic instructions; slashing the size of his army from thirty-two thousand men to ten thousand men to three hundred men (Judges 7:2–3, 7–8, 19–23). With his three hundred select men, Gideon followed God's detailed tactics to rout the Midianites. So, once again, we see the indispensable role of the Holy Spirit in this great deliverance.

## Old Testament Prophets, Priests, and Kings

Every single person the Lord used to accomplish great feats in the Old Testament had to be anointed with the Holy Spirit before embarking on their God-ordained mission. Three categories of leaders were anointed with the Holy Spirit in the Old Testament: prophets, priests, and kings. None of the Old Testament prophets spoke by their own will, but these "holy men of God spoke as they were moved by the Holy Spirit" (2 Pet. 1:21 KJV). The Greek word translated "moved" suggests the idea of being carried along. Thus, the Old Testament prophets were literally carried along by the Holy Spirit as they spoke God's words. As someone who has had the privilege of being used by God to utter prophetic messages, I can testify how wonderful this experience is. God literally puts His words in your mouth and speaks through you. Afterward, I was amazed at the wonderful, prophetic words that proceeded out of my mouth because prior to speaking them, I had no knowledge about them.

Similarly, all the high priests and the priests in the Old Testament had to be anointed with oil (symbolic of the Holy Spirit) before commencing their priestly duties. Moses "poured some of the anointing oil on Aaron's head and anointed him, to consecrate him" (Lev. 8:12 NIV). It was the anointing of the Holy Spirit upon the lives of Aaron, his sons, and their descendants that enabled them to perform their priestly ministry, which included offering sacrifices to God on behalf of the people of Israel, interceding for the people in prayer, and teaching God's Word to the people of Israel.

The kings of Israel were also anointed with oil to equip them with wisdom for administrative purposes, judgment for adjudicating cases, and supernatural strength for military adventurism and. Here are some examples:

*The Holy Spirit*

Then Samuel took a flask of oil and poured it on his head, and kissed Saul and said: "Is it not because the LORD has anointed you commander over His inheritance? ... *Then the Spirit of God came upon him* and he prophesied. (1 Sam. 10:1, 10 NKJV, emphasis mine)

The LORD said, "Arise, anoint him; for this is the one!" Then Samuel took the horn of oil and anointed him in the midst of his brothers; *and the Spirit of the LORD came upon Davi*d from that day forward (1 Sam. 16:13 NKJV, emphasis mine)

As Elijah's earthly prophetic ministry drew to a close, the LORD commanded, *"Anoint Jehu ... king over Israel, and anoint Elisha ... to succeed you as prophet"* (1 Kings 19:16 NIV, emphasis mine).

Joshua, Moses's successor and a great military leader who led the Israelites to the Promised Land and to occupy it, had to receive the Holy Spirit before embarking on his assignment.

> *Remember*
>
> *The Spirit of the Lord coming upon Gideon drastically transformed him from a coward into a mighty military leader.*

Now, Joshua, son of Nun, was *filled with the spirit of wisdom* because *Moses had laid his hands on him.* So, the Israelites listened to him and did what the LORD had commanded Moses" (Deut. 34:9 NIV, emphasis mine)

Here, we see that another way by which people could receive the Holy Spirit was through the laying on of hands. The expression "the spirit of wisdom" is a synonym for the presence of the Holy

Spirit on Joshua. Thus, the secret of Joshua's success as a leader was the anointing of the Holy Spirit upon him, which he received when Moses laid hands on him.

The secret of David's success as Israel's beloved king, prophet extraordinaire, and anointed psalmist was the Spirit of God that rested on him (2 Sam. 23:1–2). All the prophets of old were anointed by the Holy Spirit. The words they wrote and spoke did not originate from them but from the Holy Spirit, who breathed on them (2 Peter 1:21). In the same way, we can only be truly successful in our calling as Christians if we are continually filled and led by the Holy Spirit.

**Chapter Takeaway**

We must be filled with the Holy Spirit to walk faithfully with God.

- God sets aside each person He chooses to use by filling them with His Holy Spirit.
- God never intends anyone to do His work without first being filled with His Holy Spirit.

**Reflective Response**

- Though Enoch was a prophet, what really distinguished him from everyone else was "he walked with God" (Gen. 5: 21–24). What does that mean to you?
- Do you have a burning desire to walk with God? If yes, what helpful tips can you glean from Enoch's life? If no, why?
- Choose any three Old Testament personalities—a king, a priest, a prophet, and a judge. Write down how the anointing of the Holy Spirit on each of them made a difference in their calling.
- The Spirit of God upon Bezalel gave him outstanding skills of craftsmanship. What life applications can you draw from this?

- When the Holy Spirit came upon Gideon, he was totally transformed from a weakling into a mighty military leader. What lessons can you learn from his experience—and how can you apply them to your life?
- What other lessons have you learned from these Old Testament leaders with respect to the indispensable role the Holy Spirit played in their lives?

## Chapter 6

### Indispensable in the Life and Ministry of Jesus

*How God anointed Jesus of Nazareth with the Holy Spirit and with power, who went about doing good and healing all who were oppressed by the devil, for God was with Him.*
—Acts 10:38 (NKJV)

Unlike any other man that lived before Him and after Him, Jesus came on earth to fulfill all that was written about Him in the scriptures (Ps. 40:7). As many as 354 prophecies were recorded about Him several hundreds of years before His incarnation, and every one of them was fulfilled with amazing precision during his short life time on earth. The prophecies encompassed every aspect of His earthly life: birth, ministry, death, and resurrection.

The golden thread that ran through all the prophecies about

> **Remember**
>
> *Every aspect of Jesus's life and ministry was propelled by the power of the Holy Spirit.*

Jesus was the vital role of the Holy Spirit in His life. Though He was 100 percent God and 100 percent man, Jesus had to operate in the power of the Holy Spirit while on earth. Every aspect of His life and ministry was empowered and propelled by the Holy Spirit. The entire ministry of Jesus, including his teaching, preaching, healing, working of miracles, and casting out demons, was empowered by the Holy Spirit.

## Indispensable in Jesus's Incarnation

When the angel Gabriel came to a young virgin named Mary to tell her she was going to be the mother of the promised Messiah, he explained to her how this supernatural event would take place.

> And the angel answered and said to her, "The Holy Spirit will *come upon you*, and the power of the Highest will *overshadow* you; therefore, also, that Holy One who is to be born will be called the Son of God." (Luke 1:35 NKJV, emphasis mine)

Gabriel predicted that the Holy Spirit would come upon Mary and overshadow her in much the same way that the Holy Spirit had hovered over the earth at creation to bring about order. Consequently, Mary's conception of Jesus would be a supernatural act, and Jesus would literally be the Son of God (not son of Joseph). In other words, Jesus would be a man into whom God's DNA would be impacted by the Holy Spirit. No other man possessed this unique combination and characteristic.

## Sign of Messiahship

The prophet Isaiah prophesied about Jesus more than any other prophet. He recorded 124 prophecies about Jesus's first coming, most of which pointed to Jesus as the one God had anointed with the Holy Spirit to set people free:

> The Spirit of the Sovereign LORD is on me, because the LORD has anointed me to proclaim good news to the poor. He has sent me to bind up the brokenhearted, to proclaim freedom for the captives and release from darkness for the prisoners. (Isa. 61:1 NIV)

In the Nazareth synagogue, Jesus read this very passage in Isaiah. When He was done, He closed the scroll and announced to the congregants, "Today this scripture is fulfilled in your hearing" (Luke 4:21 NKJV). In plain English, Jesus told them, "I am the one Isaiah prophesied about."

Jesus revealed to His fellow Nazarenes that the LORD had anointed Him with the Holy Spirit to do four things: proclaim good news to the poor, bind up the brokenhearted, proclaim freedom for the captives, and release from darkness for the prisoners. In other words, He had come to preach the good news of the kingdom of God, heal the sick, teach, and deliver those who are bound by satanic power. In order to fulfill these ministries, Jesus *had* to be anointed with the Holy Spirit, making the anointing of the Holy Spirit on Jesus indispensable for His earthly ministry.

Several other prophetic utterances point to the fact that Jesus would be filled with the Holy Spirit. For example, Jesus's divine characteristics were prophesied about seven hundred years before His incarnation:

> A shoot will come up from the stump of Jesse; from his roots a Branch will bear fruit. The Spirit of the LORD will rest on Him, the spirit of wisdom and understanding, the spirit of counsel and strength, the spirit of knowledge and the fear of the LORD. (Isa. 11:1–2 NIV)

The metaphor "a shoot from the stump of Jesse" means a descendant of Jesse. Jesus was the descendant of Jesse who perfectly fulfilled that prophecy (Matt. 1:5–6). The divine attributes mentioned in Isaiah 11:2 attest to the fact that the Messiah (Jesus) would not operate in his own power but in the fullness of the Holy Spirit.

God promised to anoint and empower Jesus with the Holy Spirit:

> Here is my servant, whom I uphold, my chosen one in whom I delight; I will put my Spirit on him." (Isa. 42:1 NIV)

This prophesy sounds very much like the words the Father spoke as Jesus came out of the water after His baptism by John:

> When all the people were baptized, it came to pass that Jesus also was baptized; and while He prayed, the heaven was opened. And the Holy Spirit descended in bodily form like a dove upon Him, and a voice came from heaven which said, "You are My beloved Son; in You I am well pleased." (Luke 3:21–22 NIV)

As discussed in chapter 4 of this book and clearly stated in Luke 3:21, the dove that descended on Jesus symbolized the Holy Spirit. Luke's account of this event is unique in the sense that he is the only Gospel writer who reported about Jesus praying after His baptism. It makes me wonder whether the Holy Spirit came upon Jesus in response to His prayer. I don't know the answer to that, but it begs the question, If even Jesus found the need to constantly engage Himself in prayer and depend on the Holy Spirit, how much more do we need to?

Though Jesus was the beloved Son of God, yet because of His fear of God and submission to His Father's will, He earnestly prayed "with vehement cries and tears ... and He was heard because of His obedience" (Heb. 5:7–8 NKJV). Prayer affords us a unique opportunity to exchange our weakness for the Lord's supernatural power. Submission to God's will is essential for enjoying continuing fellowship with the Holy Spirit. Jesus's example of total obedience to the Father should teach us to do same.

## Baptizer in the Holy Spirit

Prior to Jesus's baptism, John the Baptizer had introduced Jesus as the baptizer in the Holy Spirit.

> The people were waiting expectantly and were all wondering in their hearts if John might possibly be the Messiah. John answered them all, "I baptize you in water. But one who is more powerful than I will come, the straps of whose sandals I am not worthy to untie. He will baptize you in the Holy Spirit and fire." (Luke 3:15–16 NIV)

This ministry of Jesus as the baptizer in the Holy Spirit distinguished Him from any other prophet who had preceded Him and would come after him. It is the exclusive preserve of Jesus to baptize believers in the Holy Spirit. The importance of this distinct feature of Jesus's ministry as the baptizer in the Holy Spirit is underscored by the fact that it is recorded in all four Gospels (Matt. 3:13–17; Mark 1:9–11; John 1:32–34). John's account of the Lord's baptism is particularly instructive in that John the Baptizer explained to his questioners that the distinguishing feature that enabled him identify Jesus as the Messiah was the Holy Spirit coming upon Him.

> The next day John saw Jesus coming toward him and said, "Look, the Lamb of God, who takes away the sin of the world! This is the one I meant when I said, 'A man who comes after me has surpassed me because he was before me.' I myself did not know him, but the reason I came baptizing with

(in) water was that he might be revealed to Israel." Then John gave this testimony: "I saw the Spirit come down from heaven as a dove and remain on him. And *I myself did not know him, but the one who sent me to baptize with (in) water told me, 'The man on whom you see the Spirit come down and remain is the one who will baptize with (in) the Holy Spirit.'* I have seen and I testify that this is God's Chosen One." (John 1:29–34 NIV, emphasis mine; "in" is alternate translation for "with.")

In this account, John made five great points. First, Jesus (not John) was the promised Messiah. Second, Jesus would be a redeeming or sacrificial Messiah (as signified by the phrase "Lamb of God"). Third, the distinguishing mark of Jesus's Messiahship would be His ministry as baptizer in the Holy Spirit. Four, John could identify Jesus as Messiah if he saw the sign God had given him—i.e. the Holy Spirit coming down and remaining on Jesus. Fifth, the entire ministry of John was to reveal and bear witness to Jesus as God's Chosen Messiah.

It is important to note that Jesus did not exercise His ministry as baptizer in the Holy Spirit during His earthly ministry. He only did so after His ascension to heaven and exaltation at the right hand of the Father. In explaining the first experience of the baptism in the Holy Spirit, Peter declared on the day of Pentecost that the exalted Christ "has received from the Father the promised Holy Spirit and has poured out what you now see and hear" (Acts 2:32 NIV). Jesus's ministry as baptizer in the Holy Spirit and fire is one of the two ministries He (Jesus) has right now; the other ministry is our advocate or intercessor (1 John 1:5; Romans 8:34).

## Strengthener in Temptation

Immediately after His baptism, the Holy Spirit led Jesus into the wilderness to be tempted by Satan. This is how Mark reported it:

> Immediately *the Spirit drove Him* into the wilderness. And He was there in the wilderness forty days, tempted by Satan, and was with the wild beasts; and the angels ministered to Him. (Mark 1:12–13 NKJV, emphasis mine)

The idea of the Holy Spirit "driving or leading" Jesus into the wilderness to be tempted by the devil (Mark1:12; Matt. 4:1) is the same as how the prophets of old were "moved" to write the scriptures. Jesus, like the Old Testament prophets, was "carried along" by the Holy Spirit into the wilderness to be tempted by the devil. The language used by the Gospel writers signifies the idea that Jesus's temptation had to take place. It was a necessity. The Holy Spirit led Jesus into the wilderness for one purpose: to be tempted by Satan.

Not only did the Holy Spirit lead Jesus into the wilderness to be tempted by Satan, but He also strengthened Jesus during His (Jesus's) temptation in the wilderness. This teaches us that the Holy Spirit could lead us out of our comfort zone to places and situations where our faith would be severely challenged, but in those trying situations, He would definitely show up to strengthen us.

**Power for Ministry**

After His temptation, Jesus launched into a three-year ministry of a kind the world had never seen. He taught with authority.

> The crowds were amazed at His teaching; because *He taught as one who had authority*, and not as their teachers of the law. (Matt. 7:28–29 NIV, emphasis mine)

He also performed spectacular miracles that stunned those who saw them:

> Coming to his hometown, He (Jesus) began teaching the people in their synagogue, and they were amazed. "Where did this man get this wisdom and these miraculous powers?" they asked. (Matt. 13:54 NIV)

The four Gospels record thirty-seven miracles that Jesus performed, including healing of a blind, mute, and deaf (Matt. 12:22–23), walking on the sea (Mark 6:45–52), and raising of Lazarus from the dead (John 11:1–45).

> Jesus did many other things as well. If every one of them were written down, I suppose that even the whole world would not have room for the books that would be written. (John 21:25 NIV)

Another important aspect of Jesus's ministry was casting out demons:

> And He healed many who were sick with various diseases, and cast out many demons. And He would not permit the demons to speak, because they knew Him. (Mark 1:34 ESV)

The entire ministry of Jesus is summed up in one sentence:

> How God anointed Jesus of Nazareth with the Holy Spirit and power, and how He went around doing good and healing all who were under the power of the devil, because God was with Him. (Acts 10:38 NIV)

The source of the power of Jesus's ministry was the Holy Spirit. The Holy Spirit was the indispensable helper in Jesus's entire ministry—teaching, preaching, healing, performing miraculous acts, and casting out demons.

In John 3:34, the Bible says Jesus spoke God's words because God gave Him the Spirit without measure. During the few days preceding his Crucifixion, Jesus spent a great of time assuring His disciples that it was to their advantage that He was going away because He was going to send them another Helper, whose presence would be more beneficial than His physical presence (John 14:15–31; 16:5–15). He also assured them that the Holy Spirit would be in them an ever-refreshing and overflowing river (John 7:37–39).

Another indispensable role the Holy Spirit played in Jesus's life was He enabled Jesus to redeem us from the power of sin.

> How much more, then, will the blood of Christ, who through the eternal Spirit offered himself unblemished to God, cleanse our consciences from acts that lead to death, so that we may serve the living God! (Heb. 9:14 NIV)

### Imparter of Life

The Holy Spirit also raised Jesus from the dead:

> And if the Spirit of him who raised Jesus from the dead is living in you, he who raised Christ from the dead will also give life to your mortal bodies because of his Spirit who lives in you. (Rom. 8:11 NIV)

Given the fact that death is the final enemy that will be defeated at the resurrection of the saints, the Holy Spirit's role in raising Jesus from the dead is a huge one. Can you imagine what would have happened if Jesus had not been raised from the dead? There would be no Christianity, no forgiveness of sin, no hope, and no sending of the Holy Spirit. Our faith in Christ would be dead, and Christians would be the most miserable people on earth.

> And if Christ has not been raised, your faith is futile; you are still in your sins. Then those also who have fallen asleep in Christ are lost. If only for this life we have hope in Christ, we are of all people most to be pitied. (1 Cor. 15:17–19 NIV)

Thank God for the indispensable work the Holy Spirit did by raising Christ from the dead! Today, the same Holy Spirit, who raised Christ from the dead, also heals our physical bodies (Rom. 8:11). Hallelujah!

The Holy Spirit raised Christ from the dead, and He also continued to empower Him during His post-resurrection ministry (Acts 1:2). One of the most important themes Jesus taught His disciples after His resurrection was the promise of the Father. A few days before His ascension, Jesus said these words to His disciples:

> I am going to send you what my Father has promised; but stay in the city until you have been clothed with power from on high. (Luke 24:49 NIV)

> On one occasion, while he was eating with them, he gave them this command: "Do not leave Jerusalem, but wait for the gift my Father promised, which you have heard me speak about." (Acts 1:4 NIV)

The point Jesus was making was this: "When I return to my Father, I will ask Him (the Father) for the promised Holy Spirit, and when I receive Him (the Holy Spirit), I will send Him (the Holy Spirit) to you." This promise was fulfilled on the day of Pentecost.

## Chapter Takeaway

The Holy Spirit played an indispensable role in the life and ministry of Jesus.

- Jesus did not do anything (ministry wise) until the Holy Spirit came upon Him in visible form at His baptism.
- Jesus withstood Satan's temptation through the power of the Holy Spirit, taught with authority, performed miracles, and cast out demons, all through the anointing of the Holy Spirit.

## Devotional Response

- The earthly ministries of Jesus comprised teaching, preaching, healing, and casting out demons. John the Baptist identified another ministry of Jesus as baptizer in the Holy Spirit. Did Jesus demonstrate this ministry as baptizer in the Holy Spirit while on earth?
    - If yes, describe when?
    - If no, why?
- What are the two main ministries of Jesus right now? Hint: Acts 1:4; 1 John 1:5. How can you benefit from these wonderful ministries of Jesus?
- If Jesus, the Second Person of the Trinity in human form, needed the anointing of the Holy Spirit, how much will His followers need it? Discuss.

# Chapter 7

## Indispensable in the First-Century Church

*All human efforts, including careful planning, promotional drives, and human expertise, will never yield God-approved results unless those efforts are Christ-initiated, Holy Spirit-empowered, and God-glorifying.*

THE TIME WAS 8:45 a.m. The temple was packed to capacity. Devout Jews and non-Jew proselytes had come from all over the world to celebrate the Hebrew festival of Shavu'oth or Feast of Weeks, which was celebrated seven weeks after the Feast of Passover (Exo. 34:22; Deut. 16:10). In Greek, the feast was known as Pentecost, meaning fiftieth, because it occurred on the fiftieth day after Passover. As required by Law, the high priest presented sacrifices, gifts, and offerings to the LORD on his own behalf and on behalf of all the people.

A few blocks from the temple, 120 disciples of Jesus had gathered in the Upper Room to pray for the Promised Holy Spirit and study the scriptures in obedience to the Lord's instruction.

Before His ascension into heaven, the Lord Jesus Christ had given His disciples this command:

> Do not leave Jerusalem, but wait for the gift my Father promised. For John baptized with *(alternate translation: in)* water, but in a few days you will be baptized with *(alternate translation: in)* the Holy Spirit. ... You will receive power when the Holy Spirit comes on you; and you will be my witnesses in Jerusalem, and in all Judea and Samaria, and to the ends of the earth. (Acts 1:4–5, 8 NIV, emphasis mine)

How could the Lord entrust the responsibility of world evangelization to these fearful, unlearned men? They had no influence, no name recognition, and no money. To make matters worse, they repeatedly doubted the resurrection of their master (Mark 16:11; Luke 24:11) and were at a loss about their own future security (Acts 1:5). Yet, it was to these helpless, hopeless, and weak people that the all-wise Lord entrusted the awesome responsibility of world evangelization. Without doubt, the responsibility was much bigger than them. The resources for getting the job done were out of this world—literally. To say that they lacked the ability, skills, education, and financial resources for the work (not talking about their personal sustenance) is an understatement.

Undoubtedly, God had chosen the "foolish folks" of this world to confound the wise and the powerless people in this world to shame the strong. He had chosen the insignificant and despised people to shut down the boastings of the arrogant and self-righteous (1 Cor. 1:26–31). God designed it this way so that in the end, no man may boast in His presence (1 Cor. 29).

Despite the daunting limitations that faced these disciples, they had one thing going for them: their obedience to their departed Master. In obedience to the Lord's command, they chose to forgo the festivities of Pentecost to seek the Helper they could not do without. They forsook the temple made with human hands in order to prepare their hearts to be the temple made without hands. The more they prayed, the thirstier they became for the living streams of the Holy Spirit (John 7:37–39). The more they travailed in prayer, the hungrier they became for the Spirit who alone could satisfy their hunger. Though unsure of the exact date the Holy Spirit would come and the form the impartation would take, these 120 disciples waited in obedience and great expectation.

Ten days of prayer and study of the scriptures culminated in unity of purpose, drive, and vision. These 120 disciples did not seek fame, recognition, or human acceptance. They wanted only one thing: power to be effective witnesses for the Lord (Acts 1:8). They craved for power to testify about the One they had heard with their ears, seen with their eyes, and touched with their hands (1 John 1:1). They wanted to be instruments through whom the Gospel of the kingdom could be proclaimed to the world (Acts 4:29–30). They were ready to obey the Lord's command to go to the entire world and proclaim "repentance for the forgiveness of sins in Jesus's name (Mark 16:15 NIV), but first they had to be "clothed with power from on high" (Luke 24:47, 49 NIV). As they prayed in one accord:

> *Remember*
>
> *The disciples did not seek fame, recognition, or acceptance. They wanted only one thing: power to be effective witnesses for the Lord.*

> Suddenly, there was a sound from heaven like the roaring of a mighty windstorm, and it filled the house where they were sitting. Then, what looked like flames or tongues of fire appeared and settled on each of them. And everyone present was filled with the Holy Spirit and began speaking in other

languages, as the Holy Spirit gave them this ability. (Acts 2:2–4 NLT)

Thus, the Church was born. It was born in power! It was born in prayer! It was born in worship and praise to God! The preparation was done in obscurity, but the launch was showcased with great spectacle. A sound from heaven, the roaring of a mighty windstorm, flames of tongues, and speaking in other tongues (Greek: glossolalia) alerted the world that God was ushering in a new era! These spectacular events attracted thousands of people to the small assembly of disciples and gave Peter and his fellows the opportunity of a lifetime to proclaim the Gospel to multitudes of curious inquirers.

God ordained that the Church should be inaugurated on Pentecost Sunday—a day when Jerusalem would be filled with people. He wanted the advent of the Holy Spirit on earth to make the maximum impact at no cost to the church. Organizing an evangelistic event for crowds of that magnitude at one location would have required elaborate preparations, including renting a huge stadium, advertising, and making complex arrangements such as seating, shelter, security, water, and toilet facilities. In His sovereignty and infinite wisdom, the Lord took care of all these logistical exigencies as the church waited on Him in obedience, and He set up the stage for Peter to proclaim the Gospel with boldness and power under the anointing of the Holy Spirit! Oh, the infinite wisdom of God, who can fathom His ways?

> **Remember**
>
> *God wanted the advent of the Holy Spirit on earth to make the maximum impact at no cost to the Church.*

Using elaborate Old Testament prophecies, Peter testified to the crowd that Jesus, who had been crucified but was raised from the dead, now seated at God's right hand, was indeed the promised

*The Holy Spirit*

Savior. "Therefore, let all Israel be assured of this: God has made this Jesus, whom you crucified, both Lord and Messiah" (Acts 2:36 NIV), Peter told them. Backed by the power of the Holy Spirit, Peter's message, like a sharp knife, cut to their hearts (Acts 2:37; John 14:24).

> When the people heard this, they were cut to the heart and said to Peter and the other apostle, "Brothers, what shall we do?" Peter replied, "Repent and be baptized, every one of you, in the name of Jesus Christ for the forgiveness of your sins. And you will receive the gift of the Holy Spirit. The promise is for you and your children and for all who are far off—for all whom the Lord our God will call." (Acts 2:37–39 NIV)

Three thousand souls repented and were baptized that day and added to the church. What a difference the Holy Spirit made in the lives of these hitherto fearful disciples. Peter, who had denied ever knowing Jesus when confronted by a maid, now boldly proclaimed Him as Lord at the risk of his life. A few days before Pentecost, these disciples did not believe in the report that Jesus had resurrected, prompting a sharp rebuke from the resurrected Christ for their lack of faith and hardness of heart (Mark 16:12–14). In fact, when Jesus explained to them the prophecy about His death and resurrection, they did not understand. The Lord had to "open their minds so they could understand the scriptures (Luke 24:45 NIV). Even on the day of Jesus's ascension,

---

**Remember**

*What a difference the Holy Spirit made in the lives and ministry of these fearful weaklings and cynics! He was their indispensable Helper just as He is to us today!*

the disciples went fishing, unsure of their future without their master. So, at the risk of sounding tautologous, what a difference the Holy Spirit made in the lives and ministry of these fearful weaklings and cynics! Undoubtedly, the Holy Spirit was their indispensable Helper just as He is to us today!

## The Early Church

The early Church existed in a very dangerous period (AD 35 to AD 325). It was a period marked by proliferation of superstition, idolatry, hedonism, materialism, and intellectualism. Not only were there city gods, national gods, and provincial gods, but individuals and households were expected to have their personal gods as well. The Roman Empire, which ruled much of the world with a ruthless hand, also had its gods, which everyone was expected to honor and worship. It was common for people to offer food to their personal and city gods before selling them in the markets.

Guests to social events such as parties, funerals, and weddings were expected to perform certain rituals in honor of their host's gods. Failing to do so was regarded as insulting the host, his household, and the entire community. It was believed that "dishonoring" the host's gods could invoke the wrath of the gods. If the "act of dishonor" was done against the empire, it was considered treasonous and punishable by death.

It was in this hostile environment that the Church was born. Thinking that the early Christians were subverting the cultural and social order of the day, the elites fought the Church with all the power, authority, and influence at their disposal. They regarded the early Christians as traitors for going against societal norms and severely persecuted them for boldly proclaiming Jesus as the only acceptable way to the one true God.

To the Gentile intellectuals, the Church's teaching of salvation through faith in a crucified Savior was foolishness. On the other side of the pendulum, the Gospel became a stumbling block to the Jews since they looked for a political Messiah. Consequently, the

*The Holy Spirit*

early Church was subjected to intense ridicule and unimaginably harsh treatments including imprisonment, public flogging, burning at the stakes, stoning, and crucifixion.

Despite these ruthless treatments at the hands of different interest groups and authorities, the early Church thrived. Indeed, the rapid growth and earth-shaking impact of the Church overwhelmed its opponents to the extent that they described the early Christians as the people who had turned the world upside down (Acts 17:6). The early Church was too hot to hold, too powerful to douse, and too efficacious to deny! The early Christians did not have university degrees in communication, yet they amazed the doctors of oratory with their extemporaneous public speaking. The majority of them did not have much formal education, yet they astonished the experts of the Law with their profound understanding and accurate interpretation of the scriptures.

> *Remember*
>
> *The Early Church was too hot to hold, too powerful to douse, and too efficacious to deny!*

> "What are we going to do with these men?" the rulers and elders of the people asked. "Everyone living in Jerusalem knows they have performed a notable sign, and *we cannot deny it*. But to stop this thing from spreading any further among the people, we must warn them to speak no longer to anyone in this name." (Acts 4:16–17 NIV, emphasis mine)

The obvious question is, What was the secret of their resilience in the face of so much opposition? What made the early Church unstoppable despite ever-increasing persecution? A study of the New Testament, particularly "The Acts of the Apostles" onward, shows that the early church, especially the first-century church, was unstoppable because the Lord Jesus was working with them through the person of the Holy Spirit. Persecution only served as the catalyst that propelled the spread of the Gospel. In every place persecution scattered them, the early disciples preached the same Gospel for which they were being persecuted because they were filled with the Holy Spirit (Acts 8:1–3).

Understanding that they were fellow workers with God, the early disciples regularly called on the Lord to imbue them with the Holy Spirit and to confirm their witness with healings and miracles in the name of the Lord Jesus (Acts 4:30). The fire of the Holy Spirit in their inner being filled them with compassion for lost souls, and the Lord honored their faith by confirming their message with the many miraculous signs that accompanied it (Acts 8:4–8; Mark 16:20). They were always quick to give God the glory for every miraculous act they performed by the power of the Holy Spirit. For example, when the Jews stood in amazement of the healing of a crippled man, Peter and John attributed the miraculous healing to the resurrected Christ who was working with and through them by the Holy Spirit.

> Peter ... said to them: "Fellow Israelites, why do you stare at us as if by our own power or godliness we had made this man walk? The God of Abraham, Isaac and Jacob, the God of our fathers, has glorified his servant Jesus ... You killed the author of life, but God raised him from the dead. We are witnesses of this. By faith in the name of Jesus, this man whom you see and know was made strong. It is Jesus's name and the faith that comes through him that has completely healed him, as you can all see." (Acts 3:12–13, 15–16 NIV)

## Characteristics of the First-Century Church

As already pointed out, there was no stopping the Church once the Holy Spirit fell on her. The early Christians, from the apostles to new converts, recognized the indispensable role of the Holy Spirit in their individual lives and corporate ministry. They understood that they had been reconciled to God and the purpose of their existence was to fulfill the ministry of reconciliation (2 Cor. 5:18–20).

Propelled by this mandate and driven by the ever-blowing wind of the Holy Spirit, the early believers paid the high price of living and suffering for the Lord as Christ's witnesses. They cared very little about personal comfort because they were persuaded that their light affliction, which was but for a moment, was working for them an incomparable weight of glory (2 Cor. 4:17).

It will be instructive for us to explore the marks that characterized the first-century Church and then ask ourselves, "How does the contemporary Church compare with the first-century Church?"

## I: Vibrant Love

The most objective mark that characterized the first-century Church was the God-kind of love (Greek agape) and sense of oneness the believers had for one another. They did everything in one accord. For example, they all engaged in continual prayer in one accord (Acts 1:14), met daily in the temple, gladly shared their food together in homes (Acts 2:46), and ate together during their Sunday fellowship sessions (Acts 20:7, 11). Moreover, the first-century believers carried one another's burdens and prayed for persecuted brethren. For instance, when the apostle Peter was arrested and put in a maximum-security prison awaiting trial and possible execution, the church in Jerusalem prayed for Peter's release, and God sent His angel to set him free (Acts 12:5). They shared a common faith and demonstrated their love for one another by distributing their possessions and properties among themselves until nobody lacked anything (Acts 2:42–47; 4:32–37).

> *All the believers were one in heart and mind.* No one claimed that any of their possessions was their own, but *they shared everything they had.* With great power, the apostles continued to testify to the resurrection of the Lord Jesus. And God's grace was so powerfully at work in them *all* that *there were no needy persons among them.* For from time to time those who owned land or houses sold them, brought the money from the sales and put it at the apostles' feet, and it was distributed to anyone who had need. Joseph, a Levite from Cyprus, whom the apostles called Barnabas (which means "son of encouragement"), sold a field he owned and brought the money and put it at the apostles' feet. (Acts 4:32–37 NIV, emphasis mine)

You couldn't have a more powerful portrait of love than this! How could thousands of believers be *one* in heart and mind and share everything they had unless the Holy Spirit had poured agape into their regenerate spirits? Verse 33 reveals the power that the Holy Spirit generates in His people when they demonstrate unity and love for one another:

> And with great ability and power the apostles were continuously testifying to the resurrection of the Lord Jesus, and great grace [God's remarkable loving kindness and favor and goodwill] rested richly upon them *all.* (Acts 4:33 AMP)

Without doubt, love was the glue that bound the early believers together in the face of sustained hostility and intense persecution. The believers understood that the Holy Spirit had shed the love of

God abroad in their hearts (Rom. 5:5), and it was up to them to live it out (Philippians 2:12). They practiced the Lord's admonishment that "it is more blessed to give than to receive" (Acts 20:35). Their love for one another marked them out as Christ's disciples in line with Jesus's prediction: "By this everyone will know that you are my disciples, if you love one another" (John 13:35 NIV).

The unflinching unity among the first-century believers was also an answer to the Lord's prayer that His disciples and future disciples would "all be one," just as the Father and the Son are one "so that the world may believe that" Jesus is indeed God's anointed Savior (John 17:21 NIV).

The end purpose of Christian love is to showcase to the world that Jesus Christ is Lord and Savior. Without a shadow of a doubt, the capacity of the early believers to love one another and live in continual unity was made possible because the Holy Spirit had planted the seed of love in their hearts when they were born again (Rom. 5:5). The believers also gave heed to the apostles' teaching to demonstrate their love for God by loving one another.

> If someone says, "I love God," but hates a Christian brother or sister, that person is a liar; for if we don't love people we can see, how can we love God, whom we cannot see? (1 John 4:20 NLT)

## II: Self-Denial

The second distinguishing mark that characterized the first-century Church was the willingness of the believers to sacrifice everything, including their very lives, for the sake of Christ. Being fully aware that the political, religious, and socioeconomic environment they were living in were intensely hostile to the Christian faith, the early believers knew and understood the risks associated with believing in Christ, living for Him, and being His witnesses. They literally faced death daily (1 Cor. 15:31). To them, the privilege of believing in Christ went hand-in-hand with suffering for Him (Philippians 1:29). They encouraged one another to be strong in faith: "We must endure many hardships to enter the kingdom of God" (Acts 14:22 Berean Study Bible); "If you are insulted because of the name of Christ, you are blessed, for the Spirit of glory and of God rests on you" (1 Pet. 4:14 NIV).

In 2 Corinthians 11:23–29, Paul describes the extreme ordeals he had to endure for Christ's sake, including floggings, near-death experiences, thirty-nine lashes (five times), beatings with rods (three times), and shipwrecks (three times). At Antioch, Paul was stoned and dragged outside the city because they thought he was dead (Acts 14:19). The apostles lived in constant possibility of death for the sake of the Lord's kingdom. Paul expressed these dangers best in 1 Corinthians 15:31, Romans 8:36, and 1 Corinthians 4:9:

> We face death every day. (1 Cor. 15:31 NIV)

> For your sake we face death all day long; we are considered as sheep to be slaughtered. (Rom. 8:36 NIV)

> I sometimes think God has put us apostles on display, like prisoners of war at the end of a victor's parade, condemned to die. We have become a spectacle to the entire world—to people and angels alike. (1 Cor. 4:9 NLT)

The early Church believers constantly reminded themselves of the Lord's saying:

> If anyone wishes to follow Me [as My disciple], he must deny himself [set aside selfish interests], and take up his cross [expressing a willingness to endure whatever may come] and follow Me [believing in Me, conforming to My example in

living and, if need be, suffering or perhaps dying because of faith in Me]. (Matt. 16:24 AMP)

Blessed are you when people insult you, persecute you and falsely say all kinds of evil against you because of me. Rejoice and be glad, because great is your reward in heaven, for in the same way they persecuted the prophets who were before you. (Matt. 5:11–12 NIV)

What was really wonderful and amazing about the willingness of the early Church to suffer and even die for the Lord Jesus was that they embraced their fate with a sense of contentment, gladness, and joy. The apostle Paul wrote,

> *But I will rejoice even if I lose my life*, pouring it out like a liquid offering to God, just like your faithful service is an offering to God. And *I want all of you to share that joy.* (Philippians 2:17 NLT, emphasis mine)

The apostles Peter and John rejoiced when they were flogged in public for Christ's sake and continued to preach the Gospel for which they were flogged:

> They called the apostles in and had them flogged. Then they ordered them not to speak in the name of Jesus, and let them go. *The apostles left the Sanhedrin, rejoicing because they had been counted worthy of suffering disgrace for the name of Jesus.* Day after day, in the temple courts and from house to house, *they never stopped teaching and proclaiming the good news* that Jesus is the Messiah. (Acts 5:40–42 NIV, emphasis mine)

In spite of repeated prophesies that Paul would suffer great affliction and possible death in Rome, the apostle was willing to subject himself to the baptism of suffering. When other believers tried to talk him out of it, his firm response was, "Why are you weeping and breaking my heart? *I am ready* not only to be bound (imprisoned), but also *to die* in Jerusalem *for the name of the Lord Jesus*" (Acts 21:13 NIV, emphasis mine).

Stephen, James (the brother of John), Paul, and Peter all paid the ultimate price for Christ's sake and for the sake of the Gospel. This almost unbelievable characteristic of self-denial distinguished the early Church from other Church eras.

### III: Total Commitment to the Great Commission

The Great Commission refers to the command the Lord Jesus gave to all his followers to spread the good news of God's kingdom to the entire world and to make disciples of those who believe the message. It is stated in various forms in all four Gospels: Matthew 28:18–20, Mark 16:15–16, Luke 24:46–47, and John 20:21

> Then Jesus came to them and said, "All authority in heaven and on earth has been given to me. Therefore go and make disciples of all nations, baptizing them in the name of the Father and of the Son and of the Holy Spirit, and teaching them to obey everything I have commanded you. And surely I am with you always, to the very end of the age." (Matt 28:18–20 NIV)

> He said to them, "Go into all the world and preach the gospel to all creation. Whoever believes and is baptized will be saved, but whoever does not believe will be condemned. And these signs will accompany those who believe: In my name they will drive out demons; they will speak in new

tongues; they will pick up snakes with their hands; and when they drink deadly poison, it will not hurt them at all; they will place their hands on sick people, and they will get well." (Mark 16:15–18 NIV)

He told them, "This is what is written: The Messiah will suffer and rise from the dead on the third day, and repentance for the forgiveness of sins will be preached in his name to all nations, beginning at Jerusalem. You are witnesses of these things. I am going to send you what my Father has promised; but stay in the city until you have been clothed with power from on high." (Luke 24:45–49 NIV)

Again Jesus said, "Peace be with you! As the Father has sent me, I am sending you." And with that he breathed on them and said, "Receive the Holy Spirit. If you forgive anyone's sins, their sins are forgiven; if you do not forgive them, they are not forgiven." (John 20:21 NIV)

When considered together, several powerful truths can be gleaned from the above scriptures with respect to the Great Commission. I will summarize them in a bulleted format for easy recall:

- The Great Commission is a *mandate* from the Lord Jesus to *all* His followers.
- The mission is defined as making disciples of people from all nations.
- The mandate comes with the promise of divine power and authority.
- Followers of Jesus can expect miraculous acts to accompany their ministry.

- The mandate allows us to exercise divine authority, including forgiveness of sins.
- The resources needed for the mission are provided in the Holy Spirit and God's Word.

To underscore the overarching importance of the Great Commission, the Lord Jesus Christ reiterated His previous directive minutes before His ascension to heaven. As a matter of fact, the Great Commission and the order to wait for the promised Holy Spirit were the last words the Lord Jesus spoke before His ascension (Acts 1:4–9). It signifies that soul winning is the most important issue on the heart of the triune God.

The Great Commission is one of the major themes in the first-century Church as recorded in the Acts of the Apostles. The first-century Church took the Great Commission literally and seriously. Wherever people lived or gathered, the early believers went there and shared their faith with them. They went and testified to the resurrection of Christ, His saving grace, and they gave people the opportunity to repent, believe in the Lord Jesus, and be baptized. Every believer in the first century was a witness. They understood that they were Christ's ambassadors (2 Cor. 5:20). As the light and salt of the earth, the first-century believers knew that they held the key to the salvation of the world and for the preservation of truth and godliness on earth (Matt. 5:13–16).

The first-century Christians obeyed the Lord's command to preach the Gospel from Jerusalem to Judea, Samaria, and to the outermost parts of the earth wholeheartedly. In Acts chapters 1–7, the believers filled Jerusalem with the Gospel; in chapters 8–12, they spread the Gospel to Judea and Samaria; in chapters 13–28, they took the Gospel to Europe, Asia Minor, and northern Africa (outermost parts of the earth). They considered themselves as bond servants of Jesus Christ (Rom. 1:1; 2 Pet. 1:1; James 1:1) and stewards of the mysteries of God (1 Cor. 4:1). So unflinching was their commitment to the Great Commission that even persecution and threats of death could not stop the first-century Christians from spreading the Gospel (Acts 8:1–4). They were determined to obey God rather than men (Acts 5:27–29; 4:19). Every believer was a witness and a worker for the Lord!

## IV: Acknowledged the Holy Spirit as their Indispensable Helper

Another feature that set the first-century Church apart was that they understood and acknowledged the Holy Spirit as their indispensable helper. The early believers acknowledged the Holy Spirit as their indispensable partner in ministry as evidenced by their willingness to wait for the Holy Spirit before beginning the Great Commission (Acts 1:13–14; 2:1–4), seeking the baptism in the Holy Spirit right after conversion (Acts 8:14–17; 19:1–6), and listening for the voice of the Holy Spirit (Acts 13:1–4). In the midst of a great spiritual awakening in Samaria, Philip obeyed the voice of the Holy Spirit and was whisked away by the Holy Spirit to minister to an Ethiopian eunuch (Acts 8:5–8; 26–40). After his conversion, Paul waited before the Lord in prayer and fasting until he was filled with the Holy Spirit before embarking on his God-ordained ministry. In all these instances, the first-century believers demonstrated their total reliance on the Holy Spirit as their indispensable partner in life and ministry.

By relying totally on the Holy Spirit, the early Church was able to discern hypocrisy as in the case of Ananias and his wife Sapphira (Acts 5:1–11), identify disciples who had been called into leadership positions (Acts 6:1–6), and commission apostolic teams (Acts 13:1–4). In the case of the commissioning of Paul's apostolic team, the Bible tells us that

> As they ministered to the Lord and fasted, *the Holy Spirit said, "Now separate to Me Barnabas and Saul for the work to which I have called them."* Then, having fasted and prayed and laid hands on them, they sent them away. So, *being sent out by*

> *the Holy Spirit,* they went down to Seleucia, and from there they sailed to Cyprus. (Acts 13:2–4 NKJV, emphasis mine)

The first-century believers understood that it was the Holy Spirit who had called and sent out Paul and Barnabas for their missionary work. The early believers were uncompromising in their insistence on making Christ and the Holy Spirit the centerpiece of their salvation, beliefs, and lifestyle. To the Galatian believers who were trying to earn their salvation again by obeying the Law, Paul asked:

> Did you *receive the Holy Spirit* by obeying the Law? Of course not! *You received the Spirit because you believed the message you heard about Christ.* How foolish can you be? After starting your Christian lives in the Spirit, why are you now trying to become perfect by your own human effort? Through Christ Jesus, God has blessed the Gentiles with the same blessing He promised to Abraham, so that we who are believers might receive the promised Holy Spirit through faith. (Gal. 3:2, 3, 14 NLT, emphasis mine)

### V: Supernatural Lifestyle

One cannot read the story of the first-century Church without being struck by the supernatural lifestyle of the believers. Every chapter of the Acts of the Apostles contains a record of a supernatural experience. You may explore it later, but here are some examples. In Acts 2:1–4; 8:14–17; 9:6; and 10:44–48, believers were filled with the Holy Spirit and spoke in tongues—and in some instances prophesied. The exalted Christ Jesus appeared to people who opposed His Church as well as His own disciples. For example, at the height of his rampage against the early Church, Saul encountered the Lord Jesus, resulting in a dramatic change in the direction of his (Saul's) life (Acts 9:3–7). On the other end of the spectrum, the Lord Jesus appeared to an obedient disciple called Ananias and instructed him to go and pray for Saul for the restoration of his sight and to be filled with Holy Spirit (Acts 9:10–16). While standing trial in Jerusalem, the Lord Jesus "stood near Paul and said, 'Take courage! As you have testified about me in Jerusalem, so you must also testify in Rome'" (Acts 23:11 NIV).

Another common supernatural experience the early Church had was seeing of visions. For instance, Cornelius, a high-ranking military leader, who was also devout, God-fearing, and generous toward the poor, received an angelic visitation in a vision which eventually led him to send for a man called Simon Peter "who would explain to him the message of salvation" (Acts 10:1–8). At that same time, the Lord was also dealing with Peter in a vision to go and minister to Cornelius (Acts10:9–16). But for this supernatural intervention, it would have been very difficult for Peter to break tradition and set foot in the home of a Gentile. Also, while being martyred for his faith in Christ, Stephen received a vision of Jesus standing at the right-hand side of God the Father (Acts 7:55–56).

Angelic interventions were also common in the early Church. For example, an angel was sent to release Peter and John from prison:

> They arrested the apostles and put them in the public jail. But during the night an angel of the Lord opened the doors of the jail and brought them out. "Go, stand in the temple courts," he said, "and tell the people all about this new life." (Acts 5:18–20 NIV)

An angel again released Peter from a maximum-security prison (Acts 12:7–10). King Herod, who made it his top priority to harass and persecute the leadership of the early Church, was killed by an angel of the Lord for abrogating to himself the glory due God alone (Acts 12:21–23).

Another extraordinary experience the early church had was supernatural earthquakes. In response to the believers' prayer to be filled with the Holy Spirit and boldness, the place where they were meeting was shaken, and they were all filled with the Holy Spirit and spoke the word of God boldly (Acts 4:31 NIV). Another supernatural earthquake took place in a Philippi jail in response to Paul and Silas's prayer and songs of praise (Acts 16:25–28).

Furthermore, the early Church regularly exercised spiritual gifts. Peter and John healed a lame man at the temple gate called Beautiful (Acts 3:1–11), many unspecified signs and wonders were performed by the apostles (Acts 5:12), and the Lord used Paul heal the father of Publius (Acts 28:7–8). Moreover, Paul restored Eutychus back to life in Ephesus (Acts 20:9–12). Also, the Holy Spirit used Paul to cast out the spirit of divination from a maid in Philippi (Acts 16:16–18) and to heal a lame man in Lystra (Acts 14:8–10). By the anointing of the Holy Spirit, Peter healed Aeneas in Samaria (Acts 9:32–35) and raised Dorcas from the dead (Acts 9:36–42), and Philip cast out demons and performed miraculous acts in Samaria (Acts 8:7; 13).

> God did extraordinary miracles through Paul, so that even handkerchiefs and aprons that had touched him were taken to the sick, and their illnesses were cured and the evil spirits left them. (Acts 19:11–12 NIV)

Finally, it is important to state that supernatural experiences in the early Church were not always pleasant. They were sometimes harsh and quick. For example, the Holy Spirit executed supernatural judgment on the hypocritical duo, Ananias and Sapphira (Acts 5:5–10), for lying to God, the Holy Spirit. Empowered by the Holy Spirit, the apostle Paul pronounced a curse on Elymas, a magician who was hindering the proclamation of the Gospel (Acts 13:8–12).

Similarly, the apostle Peter pronounced a curse on Simon, the sorcerer, for offering money in exchange for the ability to impart the Holy Spirit (Acts 8:18–23).

VI. Unquestioned Acceptance of the Authority of scripture

Empowered by the Holy Spirit, our first-century heroes of faith accepted the scriptures as the unquestioned revelation of God to humankind. The scriptures were the bedrock of their faith, and they unashamedly upheld the authority of scripture. Throughout the New Testament, we see leading men such as Peter, John, Stephen, Philip, and Paul, extensively from the Old Testament scriptures. For example, on the day of Pentecost, the apostle Peter preached extensively from the Old Testament scriptures: Joel 2:28–30; Joel 1–3, Isaiah 2:2–21; 3:184:6; 10:20–23, Hosea 1–2, Psalms, and Amos 8:9–11; 9:9–12. Because Peter preached, proclaiming his belief in the authority of the scriptures, three thousand souls were added to the kingdom that day!

Again, when Peter and John were arraigned before the Sanhedrin and were questioned about the authority of their message and ministry, Peter pointed to the exclusively to the authority of scripture.

> And it came to pass, on the next day, that their rulers, elders, and scribes, as well as Annas the high priest, Caiaphas, John, and Alexander, and as many as were of the family of the high priest, were gathered together at Jerusalem. And when they had set them in the midst, they asked, *"By what power or by what name* have you done this?" Then *Peter, filled with the Holy Spirit,* said to them, "Rulers of the people and elders of Israel: If we this day are judged for a good deed done to a helpless man, by what means he has been made well, let it be known to you all, and to all the people of Israel, that by the name of Jesus Christ of Nazareth, whom you crucified, whom God raised from the

> dead, by Him this man stands here before you whole. This is the *'stone which was rejected by you builders, which has become the chief cornerstone.'* Nor is there salvation in any other, for there is no other name under heaven given among men by which we must be saved." (Acts 4:5–12 NKJV, emphasis mine)

Peter's statement in verse 11 is a quotation from Psalm 118:22. Moreover, the apostle Peter's two epistles make several references to Old Testament scriptures, including Deuteronomy, Jeremiah, Daniel, Leviticus, Exodus, Proverbs, Isaiah, Psalms, Hosea, Ezekiel Genesis, and Esther. Similarly, when accused of heresy, Stephen presented a strong defense of the Gospel by alluding to the authority of scripture. He traced the history of the common faith he and his accusers shared through their ancestry from Abraham and how that covenant had culminated in the coming of the Messiah, Jesus of Nazareth.

Wherever Paul preached in synagogues, he testified from the Old Testament scriptures. For instance, in Thessalonica,

> Paul went into the synagogue, and on three Sabbath days he reasoned with them from the scriptures, explaining and proving that the Messiah had to suffer and rise from the dead. (Acts 17:2–3 NIV)

Because the Gospel is the power of God unto salvation (Rom. 1:16), some of them were persuaded, and a great multitude of the devout Greeks, and not a few of the leading women, joined Paul and Silas (Acts 17:4 NKJV).

In 1 Corinthians chapter 15, Paul made a strong case for the resurrection of Christ and all believers "according to the scriptures." Paul also alluded to special revelations the Lord Jesus gave him, which later became part of the inspired Word of God. The apostle John received direct revelation from the Lord Jesus, which is now part of the scriptures as the book of Revelation. The early believers also trusted in the written Word and sought to verify everything that the apostles taught them by searching the scriptures themselves.

The Bible speaks of the "noble" Berean Jews who "received the message with great eagerness and examined the scriptures every day to see if what Paul said was true" (Acts 17:11 NIV). They refused to blindly accept the message that the great apostle Paul preached to them as true unless the teachings could be validated by their examination of the scriptures.

## Chapter 8

### Indispensable Giver of Power

*What the Holy Spirit does is sometimes
unexplainable, but it is undeniable
because it's in your face.*

IN MY HOME, THE sole source of power is electricity. I get my heating, lighting, and hot water from electricity. This means if there's electric power outage, which rarely happens, I can't get hot water to bathe, I won't be able to use the range to cook, and the heaters cannot produce heat to keep the house warm. Moreover, the computers, printer, television, and radios in my house cannot work if my electrical source is cut. These factors make electricity an indispensable utility in my home.

Similarly, in God's house (the Church), the Holy Spirit is the indispensable "source of power." Without the Holy Spirit, the Church—and by extension, believers—have no "power source." In other words, without the Holy Spirit, the Church will not have spiritual illumination and will, therefore, grope in spiritual darkness. It takes the Holy Spirit to open the eyes of our understanding to comprehend the hidden treasures buried within the pages of scripture (Ps. 119:18; Eph. 1:18). Without the Holy

Spirit, the Church will not experience "spiritual heat." The Church will be "cold" and "dry" if it does not recognize the Holy Spirit as its "power source" and allow the Spirit to do His work in our midst. Moreover, without the Holy Spirit, the Church will not know how to partner with God to fulfill His end-time purposes.

Thank God that He has not left His Church without power. The same power of the Holy Spirit that worked in the Old Testament saints, our Lord Jesus, and the early Church is available to us today (Eph. 3:20). If this "great cloud of witnesses" needed the power of the Holy Spirit to fulfill God's purposes in their generations, we cannot need less. We must accept and appropriate the Lord's promise, "You will receive power when the Holy Spirit comes on you" (Acts 1:8 NIV).

An integral part of the Great Commission package says,

> These miraculous signs will accompany those who believe: They will cast out demons in my name, and they will speak in new languages. They will be able to handle snakes with safety, and if they drink anything poisonous, it won't hurt them. They will be able to place their hands on the sick, and they will be healed. (Mark 16:17–18 NLT)

The Lord promised that these miraculous signs would accompany those who believe in Him. That includes anyone, anywhere, who believes. The tremendous power to perform supernatural signs is available in the Holy Spirit who lives in every child of God. Our responsibility is to believe the promise with childlike faith and appropriate it. In this chapter, we will discuss the indispensable role the Holy Spirit plays in infusing us with God's power for ministry. It's going to be an exciting journey, so please fasten your seat belts, join me with an open mind devoid of denominational prejudice, and let's get started!

## Baptism in the Holy Spirit

It is important to begin this discussion by defining the word *baptism*. The noun *baptism* is derived from the verb *baptize*, which is a transliteration of the Greek root word *baptizo*, meaning to immerse. Thus, baptism means immersion. Now, there are two ways by which a person can be immersed: either by submersion (dipping the person completely in the medium of baptism) or outpouring (pouring the medium of baptism on the person until the person is drenched). An example of submersion in the Bible is John the Baptist immersing (baptizing) Jesus in the Jordan River (Matt. 3:13–17). The experience of Cornelius and his household is an example of outpouring (Acts 10:44–48).

The Bible speaks of many different kinds of baptisms, both in the literal sense and in metaphoric sense, including water baptism, baptism in the Holy Spirit, baptism of fire, and baptism of suffering. For our purpose, however, we will focus on baptism in water and baptism in the Holy Spirit. It is also worthy of note that when the Bible speaks of baptism without any qualifiers, it refers to baptism in water. Two types of water baptisms are mentioned in the New Testament: John's baptism, which signified repentance from sin pending Christ's substitutionary death on the cross (Matt. 3:11), and Christian baptism, which signifies death to our old self and resurrection unto a new life in Christ (Rom. 6:4).

Every baptism has three significant characteristic elements: the baptizer, the medium of baptism, and the purpose of baptism. For example, in water baptism, the baptizer is the person (minister or disciple) doing the baptism, the medium of baptism is water, and the purpose is to identify with the death, burial, and resurrection of Christ (Rom. 6:3–4). In Holy Spirit baptism, the baptizer is the Lord Jesus (Luke 3:16), the medium of baptism is the Holy Spirit, and the primary purpose is to receive power that would enable the believer to be effective witness for Christ (Acts 1:8). Figure 1 below is my pictorial depiction of the characteristics of baptisms and the three elements of water and Holy Spirit baptisms.

| Characteristics of Baptisms | | | |
| --- | --- | --- | --- |
| **Type of Baptism** | Medium | Baptizer | Purpose |
| **Water Baptism** | Water | Believer/ Disciple | Identify with Christ's death, burial, and resurrection |
| **Holy Spirit Baptism** | Holy Spirit | Jesus Christ | Power to be effective witnesses for Christ |

*Figure 1: The Three Elements of Baptism*

## What Is the Baptism in the Holy Spirit?

To ensure clarity, let us first establish what we mean by the expression "baptism in the Holy Spirit." The baptism in the Holy Spirit refers to the supernatural experience of God "pouring out His Spirit on all flesh" as predicted by the prophet Joel and first fulfilled on the day of Pentecost.

> *Remember*
>
> *The baptism in the Holy Spirit is a supernatural endowment of power that enables the believer to be an effective witness for Christ.*

> And it shall come to pass afterward, that I will *pour out my Spirit* upon all flesh; and your sons and your daughters shall prophesy, your old men shall dream dreams, your young men shall see visions. Even on my servants, both men and women, I will pour out my Spirit in those days. (Joel 2:28–29 NIV, emphasis mine)

> When the day of Pentecost came, they were all together in one place. Suddenly, a sound like the blowing of a violent wind came from heaven and

> filled the whole house where they were sitting. They saw what seemed to be tongues of fire that separated and came to rest on each of them. All of them were *filled with the Holy Spirit* and began to speak in other tongues as the Spirit enabled them. (Acts 2:1–4 NIV, emphasis mine)

In response to inquiries from the crowd who had heard the disciples speaking and praising God in their own native languages, Peter declared:

> Fellow Jews and all of you who live in Jerusalem, let me explain this to you; listen carefully to what I say. These people are not drunk, as you suppose. It's only nine in the morning! No, this is what was spoken by the prophet Joel: "In the last days, God says, I will *pour out my Spirit* on all people. Your sons and daughters will prophesy, your young men will see visions, your old men will dream dreams. Even on my servants, both men and women, I will pour out my Spirit in those days, and they will prophesy." (Acts 2:14–18 NIV; emphasis mine)

The Bible does not give us a definition for the baptism in the Holy Spirit. However, based on the revelation of scripture, I will define the experience as follows: The baptism in the Holy Spirit is a supernatural impartation of power that transforms the believer to be an effective witness for Christ. In other words, the baptism in the Holy Spirit is a supernatural infusion of power that transforms timid believers to become bold witnesses for Christ. It is supernatural because what the believer does after receiving the baptism in the Holy Spirit cannot be explained by the natural human mind. It is also an infusion of power because the Holy Spirit empowers the believer to do what the believer could not if God had not imparted His supernatural grace on him.

## Outward Manifestation of the Baptism in the Holy Spirit

Throughout the New Testament, there was an outward manifestation whenever people received the baptism in the Holy Spirit. Every time people received the baptism in the Holy Spirit, they spoke in languages they had not learned or understood but were enabled to speak by the Holy Spirit (Acts 2:4). Let us examine the recorded history of the first-century Church to establish a pattern.

### I: Pentecost Day (Acts 2:1–4)

On the day of Pentecost, 120 disciples of Jesus, including Jesus's mother and siblings, spoke in tongues when they were baptized in the Holy Spirit.

> When the day of Pentecost came, they were all together in one place. Suddenly, a sound like the blowing of a violent wind came from heaven and filled the whole house where they were sitting. They saw what seemed to be tongues of fire that separated and came to rest on each of them. All of them were *filled with the Holy Spirit* and *began to speak in other tongues as the Spirit enabled them.* (Acts 2:1–4 NIV, emphasis mine)

### II: Cornelius and His Household (Acts 10:44–48)

A Roman centurion called Cornelius and his entire household spoke in tongues and praised God when the Holy Spirit fell upon them while Peter was still preaching to them about Jesus.

> While Peter was still speaking ... *the Holy Spirit fell upon all those who were listening to the message.* All the circumcised believers who came with Peter were amazed, because the gift of the Holy

Spirit had been poured out on the Gentiles also. For they were hearing them *speaking with tongues and exalting God*. Then Peter answered, "Surely no one can refuse the water for these to be baptized who have *received the Holy Spirit just as we did*, can he?" And he ordered them to be baptized in the name of Jesus Christ. Then they asked him to stay on for a few days. (Acts 10:44–48 NASB, emphasis mine)

### III: The Disciples at Ephesus (Acts 19:1–6)

Twelve disciples who had been water baptized spoke in tongues and prophesied when Paul laid his hands on them.

> While Apollos was in Corinth, Paul traveled through the interior regions until he reached Ephesus, on the coast, where he found several believers. "Did you receive the Holy Spirit when you believed?" he asked them. "No," they replied, "We haven't even heard that there is a Holy Spirit." "Then what baptism did you experience?" he asked. And they replied, "The baptism of John." Paul said, "John's baptism called for repentance from sin. But John himself told the people to believe in the one who would come later, meaning Jesus." As soon as they heard this, they were baptized in the name of the Lord Jesus. Then when Paul laid his hands on them, the Holy Spirit came on them, and they spoke in other tongues and prophesied. There were about twelve men in all. (Acts 19:1–7 NLT, emphasis mine)

I often wonder why Paul asked these disciples "Did you receive the Holy Spirit when you believed? Did he notice they lacked something? If yes, what was it? We know one thing for sure.

Whenever the Holy Spirit came upon believers, they received power and they became bold witnesses for Christ. So, could it be that Paul asked this question because he noticed they lacked the outward manifestations of the Holy Spirit, namely speaking in tongues, boldness, and power? It is also possible that they were not even born again since John's baptism did not lead to New Testament salvation. Anyway, when Paul explained the good news of the cross to them, had them baptized in water, and laid hands on them, the Holy Spirit came on them, and they spoke in other tongues and prophesied (Acts 19:6 NLT).

## IV: The Believers in Samaria (Acts 8:1–8; 14–18)

As a result of intense persecution of the first-century Church, the believers in Jerusalem were scattered throughout Judea and Samaria. Unperturbed by the persecution, the believers preached the Gospel wherever they went. Philip fled to a city in Samaria, and while there, he preached the Gospel. The Lord honored His Word with conversion and miraculous acts. Amazed by the power accompanying Philip's ministry, a sorcerer called Simon believed Philip's message and was baptized in water.

> When the apostles in Jerusalem heard that Samaria had accepted the word of God, they sent Peter and John to Samaria. When they arrived, they prayed for the new believers there that they might receive the Holy Spirit, because the Holy Spirit had not yet come on any of them; they had simply been baptized in the name of the Lord Jesus. Then Peter and John placed their hands on them, and they received the Holy Spirit. When Simon saw that the Spirit was given at the laying on of the apostles' hands, he offered them money and said, "Give me also this ability so that everyone on whom I lay my hands may receive the Holy Spirit." (Acts 8:14–17 NIV)

In this account, the Bible does not tell us that the Samarian believers spoke in other tongues when Peter and John placed their hands on the new believers. However, Simon's reaction clearly suggests that there was an outward manifestation of the Holy Spirit falling on them.

> When Simon saw that the Spirit was given at the laying on of the apostles' hands, he offered them money and said, "Give me also this ability so that everyone on whom I lay my hands may receive the Holy Spirit." (Acts 8:14–17 NIV)

Obviously, Simon did not see the Holy Spirit because spirits cannot be seen. So, what does the Bible mean by "when Simon saw that the Spirit was given at the laying on of the apostles' hands, he offered them money?" Clearly, what Simon saw was an outward manifestation of the presence of the Holy Spirit through the new believers. Based on the apostles' own experience and the pattern in the Acts of the Apostles, the recurring outward manifestation of the Holy Spirit was speaking in tongues. Fortunately for us, the same pattern continues to be the case up to the present time.

## IV: Paul's Experience (Acts 9:10–19)

After the dramatic conversion of Saul (who later became known as Paul), the Lord sent a disciple in Damascus named Ananias to go and place his hands on Saul so he (Saul) could have his eyesight restored and receive the Holy Spirit:

> Then Ananias went to the house and entered it. Placing his hands on Saul, he said, "Brother Saul, the Lord—Jesus, who appeared to you on the road as you were coming here—has sent me so that you may see again and be filled with the Holy Spirit." Immediately, something like scales fell from Saul's

eyes, and he could see again. He got up and was baptized, and after taking some food, he regained his strength (Acts 9:17–19 NIV).

In this account, the Bible describes the outward sign that accompanied the restoration of Saul's eyesight but is silent about the outward manifestation accompanying his being filled with the Holy Spirit. Later, in 1 Corinthians 14:18, Paul stated that he spoke in tongues more than all the believers in Corinth. He also sang in tongues and encouraged the Corinthian believers to do same (1 Cor. 14:14–15). Based on the pattern of the early church (salvation, water baptism, and Holy Spirit baptism) and Paul's on testimony to the Corinthian church, it is reasonable to infer that Paul did in fact speak in tongues when Ananias prayed for him to be filled with the Holy Spirit.

## How Did People Receive the Baptism in the Holy Spirit in the Bible?

Throughout the recorded history of the Church, people received the baptism in the Holy Spirit in two main ways: by the laying on of hands and by the sovereign intervention of God. As described earlier, Paul received the Holy Spirit when Ananias laid hands on him (Acts 9:11–18), the believers in Samaria received the Holy Spirit when Peter and John laid hands on them (Acts 8:14–17), and the disciples at Ephesus received the Holy Spirit when Paul laid hands on them (Acts 19:1–7). In all these instances, the baptism in the Holy Spirit was received by the laying on of hands of a believer who had already received the baptism in the Holy Spirit.

On the day of Pentecost, the Holy Spirit fell on the disciples while they were praying. It was a sovereign act of God since there was no human instrumentality (Acts 2:1–4). Also, in Cornelius's house (as already discussed), the Holy Spirit fell on Cornelius and his entire household while Peter was still speaking the Good News to them (Acts 10:44–46). Here again, Peter and his entourage had absolutely no hand in this supernatural act of God. In fact, it took this sovereign intervention of God to convince Peter, his entourage, and later the apostles in Jerusalem, that God does not discriminate or show favoritism with his gifts but accepts anyone who fears him irrespective of race or ethnicity (Acts 10:34–35).

In my ministry and other ministries I have been part of, I have seen believers receive the baptism in the Holy Spirit in the same way the early believers did: either by laying on of hands or by a sovereign act of God. Over the years, I have seen hundreds of people receive the baptism in the Holy Spirit when I laid hands on them; some of them were as young as ten years old. I have also witnessed many people receive the baptism in the Holy Spirit without the laying on of hands. I know some people who received the baptism in the Holy Spirit and spoke in tongues during their own private times of prayer and worship. I have also seen people receive the baptism in the Holy Spirit during corporate prayer meetings without anyone laying hands on them.

I recall a remarkable experience in 2002 where two women received the baptism in the Holy Spirit while I was baptizing them in water. During the pre-baptism teachings, I had prepared them to expect a supernatural experience during the baptism. The first one came out of the water speaking in tongues and praising God. The second lady's experience was even more dramatic. She came out of the water speaking in tongues, and she was healed of a deformed arm. So, whether one receives the Holy Spirit baptism by the laying on of hands or by a sovereign initiative, the common denominator is Jesus is the Baptizer, and He will always show up whenever we are ready and willing to let Him do His work.

If you are a believer in Jesus Christ and have not experienced the blessing of the baptism in the Holy Spirit, you can receive it right now. You don't need to "tarry" for the Holy Spirit. After Pentecost, nobody had to wait for the Holy Spirit baptism. They simply opened up to God and received the Holy Spirit baptism by faith. Also, you don't have to beg God for the Holy Spirit for two reasons. First, you don't beg your Father for a gift He has promised you.

> *The promise (of the Holy Spirit), is unto you,* and to your children, and to all that are afar off, even as many as the LORD our God shall call. (Acts 2:39 KJV, emphasis mine)

Second, you don't beg God for a blessing He wants to give you.

> If you sinful people know how to give *good gifts* to your children, *how much more will your heavenly Father give the Holy Spirit to those who ask Him?* (Luke 11:13NLT, emphasis mine)

Jesus wants you to disabuse your mind of any thoughts that God might not want you to receive the baptism in the Holy Spirit. He calls the Holy Spirit a "good gift," and as a child of God, you are entitled to your Father's good gifts. Your responsibility is to ask your Father for this gift. Ask God in faith and receive this good gift. Double-mindedness can be a hindrance to receiving the Holy Spirit baptism (James 1:5–6).

If you are thirsty for the Holy Spirit baptism with the evidence of speaking in tongues, your blessing is only a prayer away. Your heavenly Father is more than willing to give you this awesome gift. All you have to do is to acknowledge your need for the Holy Spirit baptism and ask God for it. He has promised to give you His Spirit and He will keep His Word. So, go ahead and ask Him in faith. You don't need to miss out on this blessing.

## Why Speak in Tongues?

I used to ask myself, "What difference will speaking in tongues make in my life?" After all, I was born again and maturing in Christ, was in leadership, and the Lord was using me to win souls and discipling the convicts. Well, the Bible gives us several reasons why speaking in other tongues is something worth having. Here are a few:

## I: God Wants All Christians to Speak in Tongues

One way God demonstrates His will is in the things He initiates or approves. Throughout the recorded history of the first-century Church, every case of believers receiving the Holy Spirit with the outward manifestation of speaking in tongues was either initiated by God or initiated by a disciple and approved by God (Acts 2:4; 10:44–46; 19:1–6). Now, if God initiates or approves a process, you can be sure that is His expressed will. Moreover, I believe that since all scripture is inspired by God, the apostle Paul was expressing God's mind when He said, "I would like every one of you to speak in tongues" (1 Cor. 14:5 NIV).

## II: Speaking in Tongues Sets Us on a Supernatural Plane

Speaking in tongues is a supernatural act. It sets us on a supernatural plane and gives us the ability to operate in the supernatural.

> If I pray in a tongue, my spirit prays, but my mind is unfruitful. So what shall I do? I will pray with my spirit, but I will also pray with my understanding; I will sing with my spirit, but I will also sing with my understanding. (1 Cor. 14:14–15 NIV)

Speaking in tongues gives us the capacity to communicate with Abba, Father, both with our natural minds and with our individual human spirits. It allows us to operate both in the natural realm and the supernatural realm. Praying and worshipping God with our minds alone limits us to the natural realm. When we speak in tongues, we relate to God at the spirit-to-spirit level. Jesus said this is God's prescribed worship:

> But the hour is coming, and now is, when the true worshipers will worship the Father in spirit and truth; for the Father is seeking such to worship

Him. God is Spirit, and those who worship Him must worship in spirit and truth (John 4:23–24 NKJV).

## III: Speaking in Tongues Gives Us Special Access to God

Speaking in tongues is called a prayer language for a good reason. It gives us special access to God in prayer. We speak mysteries to God when we speak in tongues, and the Holy Spirit helps us pray in line with God's will when we speak in tongues (1 Cor. 4:2). The Bible assures us that though we don't understand what we say in tongues, God does and gives us the answers we need (Rom. 8:26–27).

## IV: Speaking in Tongues Edifies Us

Speaking in tongues is a God-ordained way for believers to build themselves up spiritually: "He who speaks in a tongue edifies himself" (1 Cor. 14:4 KJV). In Jude 20, we are exhorted to build ourselves up in our most holy faith as we pray in the Holy Spirit. The apostle Paul spent a lot of time speaking in tongues in his private prayer times but in public prayer meetings, he preferred to prophesy (speak intelligible words) to edify the entire church (1 Cor. 14:18–19, 4).

## Other Thorny Issues

Another question used to bother me: "How can I be sure that if I ask God for the baptism in the Holy Spirit that what I receive is from God and not from the devil?" Well, Jesus promised us in Luke 11:13 that if we ask God for the Holy Spirit, He (God) will give us nothing but the Holy

> **Remember**
>
> *If we ask God for something, Satan cannot sneak in and give us something different.*

Spirit. If sinful parents give good gifts to their children, will our heavenly Father give us anything less? Moreover, if we ask God for something, Satan cannot sneak in and give us something different.

It took me several years after my conversion before receiving the baptism in the Holy Spirit because of conflicting teachings I received. I was a leader in the ministry and was enjoying some degree of spiritual power, but I knew there was more grace God wanted me to experience.

Ironically, I restrained myself whenever the Holy Spirit wanted to have full sway of my human spirit. For example, during an evangelistic event more than three decades ago, I saw one of the dear brothers who mentored me in the Lord. As we ran toward each other in excitement, he began to speak in tongues. In response, I felt the Holy Spirit bubbling up within me. Momentarily, I felt like speaking out in tongues, but I restrained myself. With compassion in his eyes, the brother appeared to be urging me on. "Go ahead, brother. Let go." I didn't oblige because the contrary teaching I had received was saying, "Speaking in tongues isn't for you." This is one of the reasons why I am very passionate about this issue. I want every believer to experience the full package of God's blessings, and that includes the baptism in the Holy Spirit.

In wanting God's best for you, I must also say that I am not in any way saying that the baptism in the Holy Spirit is an end in itself. Nothing could be farther from the truth. However, the baptism in the Holy Spirit gives us access to the treasure trove of God's spiritual resources for getting His work on earth done. God's spiritual treasure trove is so wide and deep that I'm not sure anyone (except Jesus) has ever fully tapped into it.

My friends who advocated the 'one-step experience' used to say "the 'two-step experience' brethren have power, but we have character (fruit)". Well, God wants us to have both. Both the power of God and Christian character are products of the Holy Spirit. Like two sides of a coin, they are complementary and not mutually exclusive. If you yield to the Holy Spirit, you will walk in His power and produce His character.

## Terminologies

The Bible uses different terminologies to describe the baptism in the Holy Spirit. As we examine a few of these terminologies, please keep in mind that the use of each terminology has its own significance in the context. Also, we know that all the different terminologies refer to the same experience. For example, John predicted that Jesus would baptize (us) in the Holy Spirit and fire (Matt. 3:11). However, when Jesus was promising this same blessing to his disciples, he said they would be clothed with power from on high (Luke 24: 49). He also promised that the disciples would be baptized in the Holy Spirit (Acts 1:5). The interesting fact is the Bible uses a variety of terms to describe the baptism in the Holy Spirit, and it is important to understand that one and the same experience is being described. Now, let us examine some of the terminologies used to describe the baptism of the Holy Spirit.

### I: Outpouring of the Holy Spirit

In Joel 2:28–29 and Acts 2:16–18, the baptism in the Holy Spirit is referred to as the LORD pouring out His Spirit on all people: sons, daughters, old people, young people, male servants, and female servants. The outward manifestation of this outpouring of the Spirit includes prophesying and Holy Spirit-inspired dreams and visions. I believe the LORD used the phrase "pour out" to paint a mental picture of immersion from on high. It pictures the Holy Spirit as a stream that flows from a hill and completely soaks the believer. It speaks of God's generosity. God does not sprinkle His Spirit on us. He pours out His Spirit on us—lavishly!

### II: Filling with the Holy Spirit

In Acts 2:4, when the 120 disciples of Jesus were baptized in the Holy Spirit, they were described as filled with the Holy Spirit:

*The Holy Spirit*

"All of them were *filled with the Holy Spirit* and began to speak in other tongues as the Spirit enabled them (Acts 2:4 NIV, emphasis mine). I understand this verse to mean that the Holy Spirit filled them to capacity and out of the abundance of their hearts, their mouth began to speak in praise to God (Luke 6:45). Similarly, when you are filled with the Holy Spirit, you won't have room for the mundane things of this world since your entire being (spirit, soul, and body) is completely yielded to the control of the Holy Spirit.

The Bible uses the expression "filled with the Holy Spirit" in two different ways. First, it is used synonymously with baptism in the Holy Spirit (Acts 1:4; Acts 9:17). When used in this sense, it refers to a one-time experience. It is also used to mean full of the Holy Spirit (Acts 4:8; 6:3, 5; 7:55) or controlled by the Holy Spirit (Eph. 5:18). It refers to the state of being under the full control of the Holy Spirit as evidenced by supernatural boldness, fruit of the Spirit, and power in proclaiming God's Word, accompanied by demonstrable signs and wonders and irresistible wisdom from God (Acts 6:5–6, 8; 7:55).

This second filling of the Holy Spirit is a continuous process. For example, the disciples were filled with the Holy Spirit in Acts 2:4. However, when they were threatened by the Jewish authorities and the church prayed, they were all filled with the Holy Spirit and preached the Word of God with boldness (Acts 4:31 NKJV).

About two decades later, the apostle Paul urged the Ephesian believers to be continuously filled with the Spirit and sing to one another in hymns and spiritual songs (Eph. 5:18–19). This means that even after being baptized in (filled with) the Holy Spirit, we must continually ask to be filled with the Holy Spirit. Why? Because we leak, as D. L. Moody famously put it.

## III: The Holy Spirit Coming Upon

In Acts 8:16; 10:44–45; 9:6; 11:15, the Bible uses the phrase "the Holy Spirit coming upon or falling upon" to describe the baptism in the Holy Spirit. Let us look at a couple of these passages. In Acts chapter 8, the Church suffers severe persecution, but that did not prevent the believers from sharing their faith wherever they went. Philip for example, fled to Samaria and preached the Gospel there. There was supernatural attestation of the Word He preached through miraculous signs and wonders. The people of Samaria received the message and were baptized (in water).

> When the apostles in Jerusalem heard that Samaria had accepted the word of God, they sent Peter and John to Samaria. When they arrived, they prayed for the new believers there that they might *receive the Holy Spirit*, because the *Holy Spirit had not yet come on* any of them; they had simply been baptized in the name of the Lord Jesus. Then Peter and John placed their hands on them, and they *received the Holy Spirit.* (Acts 8:14–17 NLT, emphasis mine)

Here, two different terminologies are used to describe the baptism in the Holy Spirit: "receiving the Holy Spirit" and "the Holy Spirit coming on" them. Again, the phrase "the Holy Spirit coming on" them signifies immersion from above. It speaks to the truth that we receive the Holy Spirit from our ascended Lord. The phrase "the Holy Spirit coming on" also signifies that the baptism in the Holy Spirit is a heavenly or supernatural experience. The phrase "receiving the Holy Spirit" reminds us that (the baptism in) the Holy Spirit is a gift we receive from God through Jesus. The responsibility of receiving the gift of the Holy Spirit lies on the individual believer and not on God who has made the gift available to us.

## IV: Receiving the Holy Spirit

It appears this is the most commonly used terminology in the first-century Church. Here are some examples:

> When they arrived, they prayed for the new believers there that *they might receive the Holy Spirit*, because the Holy Spirit had not yet come on any of them; they had simply been baptized in the name of the Lord Jesus. Then Peter and John placed their hands on them, and *they received the Holy Spirit*. (Acts 8:15–17 NIV, emphasis mine)

> While Apollos was at Corinth, Paul took the road through the interior and arrived at Ephesus. There he found some disciples and asked them, *"Did you receive the Holy Spirit when you believed?"* (Acts 9:1–2 NIV, emphasis mine)

> I would like to learn just one thing from you: *Did you receive the Spirit* by the works of the law, or by believing what you heard? (Gal. 3:2 NIV, emphasis mine)

> He redeemed us in order that the blessing given to Abraham might come to the Gentiles through Christ Jesus, so that *by faith we might receive the promise of the Spirit*. (Gal. 3:14 NIV, emphasis mine)

## V: Rivers of Living Water

Finally, Jesus described the baptism in the Holy Spirit as "streams of living water flowing from the heart."

> On the last and greatest day of the festival, Jesus stood and said in a loud voice, "Let anyone who is thirsty come to me and drink. Whoever believes in me, as scripture has said, rivers of living water will flow from within them." By this he meant the Spirit, whom those who believed in him were later to receive. Up to that time the Spirit had not been given, since Jesus had not yet been glorified. (John 7:37–39 NIV)

This passage of scripture is loaded with so much revelation that any attempt to do an exposé will be a distraction. Therefore, my intention here is not to engage in exhaustive exegesis of this passage but to point out the symbolism of the Holy Spirit as rivers of living water. The metaphor "living water" signifies life, sufficiency, and constancy. As living water, the Holy Spirit is given to us in abundance (more than we need) to provide us spiritual life and to keep us constantly fresh for the Master's use. The refreshing presence of the Holy Spirit is inexhaustible. Hallelujah!

Isn't it amazing that the LORD beckons us to come and drink freely of the inexhaustible river of the Holy Spirit (Isa. 55:1)? The question is, Will you accept the Lord's invitation and come, receive, and drink freely of the living water of the Holy Spirit? Are you thirsty enough to come and receive this gift that never runs out?

If you are thirsty, you will stop at nothing until you find water because water has no substitute. No other drink can quench your natural thirst. No amount of juice or soda can satisfy you when you are thirsty. Similarly, our spiritual thirst can only be satisfied by the living water Jesus gives: the Holy Spirit. I pray that the Lord will create in you a new craving for the Holy Spirit to make you seek Him

---

*Remember*

*Our spiritual thirst can only be satisfied by the living water Jesus gives: the Holy Spirit.*

more and more till you become all that God created you to be. Amen!

## When Does the Baptism of the Holy Spirit Occur?

Throughout the New Testament, the baptism in the Holy Spirit occurred shortly after conversion. I use the New Testament as the reference point because though the baptism of the Holy Spirit was promised in the Old Testament (Joel 2:28–29) and by the Lord Jesus (Luke 24:49; John 7:37–39), it was fulfilled on the day of Pentecost and onward. In Acts 2:38–39, the apostle Peter, by the inspiration of the Spirit, told the crowd,

> Each of you must *repent of your sins and Turn to God*, and *be baptized* in the name of Jesus Christ for *the forgiveness of your sins. Then* you will receive *the gift of the Holy Spirit. This promise is to you, and to your children, and even to the Gentiles*—all who have been called by the Lord our God. (Acts 2:38–39 NLT, emphasis mine)

The promise is for those who have repented of their sins and have received forgiveness of their sins through belief in the finished work of the Lord Jesus Christ on the cross of Calvary. Moreover, the promise of baptism in the Holy Spirit did not end with the first apostles. "The promise is for you and your children and for all who are far off—for all whom the Lord our God will call" (Acts 2:39 NIV). The phrase "all who are far off—for all whom the Lord our God will call" refers to all Gentiles and everyone living today.

### I: Jesus's Prediction

Jesus said, "Whoever believes in me, as scripture has said, rivers of living water will flow from within them" (John 7:38–39 NIV). By this, He meant the Spirit, whom those who believed in him were later to receive.

We can deduce a couple of truths from Jesus's statement. First, Jesus clearly identifies belief in Him as a condition for receiving the Holy Spirit. This means the gift of the Holy Spirit cannot be received by unbelievers. Second, Jesus said, "Rivers of living water will flow from within them." I understand this to mean the Holy Spirit, who is already residing in the believer, will become an all-sufficient, constantly flowing, never-ceasing river that touches and blesses other lives.

## II: The Experience of Jesus's Disciples

Jesus's disciples received the promised Holy Spirit subsequent to their salvation. They were born again when Jesus breathed on them individually after his resurrection and said, "Receive ye the Holy Spirit" (John 20:22 KJV). The Greek phrase translated "receive ye the Holy Spirit" suggests that the disciples did receive the Holy Spirit when Jesus breathed on them. Yet, forty days later—just before His ascension—Jesus gave His disciples this command:

> Do not leave Jerusalem, but wait for the gift my Father promised, which you have heard me speak about. For John baptized with (in) water, but in a few days you will be baptized with (in) the Holy Spirit. (Acts 1:4 NIV)

The disciples received the promised baptism in the Holy Spirit ten days after Jesus's ascension:

> When the day of Pentecost came, they were all together in one place. Suddenly a sound like the blowing of a violent wind came from heaven and filled the whole house where they were sitting. They saw what seemed to be tongues of fire that

separated and came to rest on each of them. All of them were filled with the Holy Spirit and began to speak in other tongues as the Spirit enabled them. (Acts 2:1–4 NIV)

## III: The Experience of Paul

Saul (later referred to as Paul) received the (baptism in the) Holy Spirit three days after his conversion. He was born again when he encountered the resurrected Christ on the road to Damascus, but he received the baptism in the Holy Spirit three days later when Ananias laid hands on him and prayed for restoration of his sight and for him to receive the Holy Spirit.

> For three days he was blind, and did not eat or drink anything ... Then Ananias went to the house and entered it. Placing his hands on Saul, he said, "Brother Saul, the Lord—Jesus, who appeared to you on the road as you were coming here—has sent me so that you *may see again* and *be filled with the Holy Spirit.*" Immediately, something like scales fell from Saul's eyes, and he could see again. He got up and was baptized, and after taking some food, he regained his strength. (Acts 19:9, 17–19 NIV, emphasis mine)

## IV: The Experience of the Samarian Believers

The Samarian believers received the Holy Spirit some days after their conversion:

> When the apostles in Jerusalem heard that *Samaria had accepted the Word of God*, they sent Peter and John to Samaria. When they arrived, they prayed for the new believers there that *they*

*might receive the Holy Spirit, because the Holy Spirit had not yet come on any of them*; they had simply been baptized in the name of the Lord Jesus. Then Peter and John placed their hands on them, and *they received the Holy Spirit.* (Acts 9:14–17 NIV, emphasis mine)

### V: The Experience of the Disciples at Ephesus

As previously discussed, these disciples believed in Christ, were water baptized, and then received the baptism of the Holy Spirit after Paul had laid hands on them (Acts 19:1–6). The Bible says that in the mouth of two or three witnesses, every word shall be established (2 Cor. 13:1). Therefore, the truths presented here are established.

### The Purpose of the Baptism in the Holy Spirit

Since the baptism in the Holy Spirit is God's idea and God never initiates anything without a clear-cut purpose, we can definitely be sure that God has a purpose for making provision for His children to be baptized in the Holy Spirit. There are several reasons why Jesus baptizes us in the Holy Spirit, but I will describe just a few.

### I: Power to be Effective Witnesses for Christ

The Lord Jesus tells us that the primary purpose for the baptism in the Holy Spirit is to give believers the power to be effective witnesses of Christ. Jesus says,

> You will receive power when the Holy Spirit comes on you; and you will be my witnesses in Jerusalem, and in all Judea and Samaria, and to the ends of the earth. (Acts 1:8 NIV)

It is important to note that Jesus acknowledges in this passage of scripture that we need power to be His witnesses. Why is that? This is because the Bible says we are engaged in a spiritual battle against "evil rulers and authorities of the unseen world, against mighty powers in this dark world, and against evil spirits in the heavenly places" (Eph. 6:12 NLT). The primary purpose of these powerful spiritual beings is to oppose God and His Christ and frustrate God's purposes with the goal of depriving God of His glory and honor. To accomplish his goal, Satan has blinded the minds of those who do not have a relationship with Jesus, and he jealously keeps them hostage.

> The god of this age has blinded the minds of unbelievers, so that they cannot see the light of the gospel that displays the glory of Christ, who is the image of God. (2 Cor. 4:4 NIV)

So, when we step out as Christ's witnesses, we set ourselves diametrically against Satan and his host of evil spirits. We, therefore, need to be "clothed with power from on high" (Luke 24:49) to overcome Satan's power and to free those he has kept hostage. The Lord Jesus underscored this truth as follows:

> Who is powerful enough to enter the house of a strong man like Satan and plunder his goods? Only someone even stronger—someone who could tie him up and then plunder his house. (Matt. 12:29 NLT)

We also need power for holistic ministry. The Great Commission is a holistic package involving winning the unsaved for Christ, casting out demons, healing the sick, and teaching believers to become disciples. The Lord Jesus Christ has given His church (believers in Christ) the mandate to:

> Go into all the world and *preach the gospel* to all creation. Whoever believes and is baptized will be saved, but whoever does not believe will be condemned. And these signs will accompany those who believe: In my name they will *drive out demons*; they will *speak in new tongues*; they will *pick up snakes with their hands*; and when they drink *deadly poison,* it *will not hurt them* at all; they *will place their hands on sick people, and they will get well.* (Mark 16:15–17 NIV, emphasis mine)

## II: To Glorify Christ

The second purpose of the baptism in the Holy Spirit is to glorify our resurrected and ascended Lord. Before His ascension to heaven, Jesus had predicted that when the Holy Spirit comes, "He (the Holy Spirit) will bring glory to me (Jesus) by telling you whatever He receives from me" (John 16:14 NLT). Jesus Christ has received a name that is above every other name and is occupying the most prestigious place in glory (Eph. 1:17–23), but it takes the Holy Spirit to give us a revelation of this truth.

> God has highly exalted Him (Jesus) and bestowed on Him the name which is above every name, so that at the name of Jesus every knee shall bow [in submission], of those who are in heaven and on earth and under the earth, and that every tongue will confess and openly acknowledge that Jesus Christ is Lord (sovereign God), to the glory of God the Father. (Philippians 2:9–10 AMP)

In God's infinite wisdom, He has deposited unsurpassed power in ordinary believers to show forth the glorious Christ. The baptism in the Holy Spirit gives believers the awareness and a unique

*The Holy Spirit*

revelation of the glorified Christ which enable them to enforce the purposes of God on earth.

### III: Boldness for Ministry

The baptism in the Holy Spirit gives believers a new drive, boldness, and desire to do God's will. Though the disciples of Jesus had been mentored for three and half years by no less a person than Jesus himself, they were timid and afraid to carry out the Lord's command to go and preach the Gospel. No wonder Jesus instructed them to stay in Jerusalem until they had been "clothed with power from on high" (Luke 24:49 NIV). These tails-between-legs disciples turned the world upside down when they were baptized in the Holy Spirit (Acts 17:6). The baptism in the Holy Spirit puts a new fire within believers, which make them unstoppable.

### IV: Insatiable Desire to Know God

The baptism in the Holy Spirit creates in those who receive it a craving for God that gets deeper the more they get to know God. This insatiable craving for God creates in Holy Spirit-baptized believers a strong, insatiable desire for God's Word, worship, and prayer. The more they yield to the Lordship of the Holy Spirit, the more the Holy Spirit transforms them into the image of Christ. With a fresh desire to know God comes a new sensitivity to what pleases the Holy Spirit and what grieves Him.

### V: Help in Prayer

The deeper craving for God, which we receive with the baptism in the Holy Spirit, puts a new burden for prayer and intercession on the believer. Not only does the baptism in the Holy Spirit enable the believer to pray more but the Holy Spirit *helps* the believer in prayer. Though the Bible commands us to pray with all kinds of prayer, the Bible also reveals that we are inadequate in prayer, and it takes the Holy Spirit to pray aright.

> The Holy Spirit *helps* us in our weakness. For example, we don't know what *God wants us to pray for*. But *the Holy Spirit prays for us* with groanings that cannot be expressed in words. And the Father who knows all hearts knows what the Spirit is saying, for the Spirit pleads for us believers in harmony with God's own will. (Rom. 8:26 NLT, emphasis mine)

This passage of scripture provides a clear picture of the *helping* role of the Holy Spirit in the life of the believer. For instance, He *helps us* pray in such a way as to get results. As human beings, we are limited in our ability to pray and our knowledge of what God wants us to pray about. Fortunately, the Holy Spirit knows what's on God's heart and helps us pray aright by interceding (praying) for us. The interesting thing is the Holy Spirit intercedes for us *through us* using our vocal cavity and "with groans too deep for words" (Berean Study Bible).

Nowhere is this experience more vivid than when believers pray in tongues. The Holy Spirit enables the believer to pray in a language the Holy Spirit gives, which the believer does not understand—but God does. Since this kind of prayer circumvents the believer's natural limitations and is packaged exactly in accordance with God's will, God answers the believer's prayer speedily. This wisdom of God is beautiful! It's awesome! And it's marvelous!

Figure 2 is my visual depiction of this kind of Holy Spirit-empowered prayer. First, the Holy Spirit receives and communicates God's thoughts to the believer. Second, the Holy Spirit nudges the believer to pray, but the believer does not know what to pray about or how to pray. Third, the Holy Spirit enables the believer to pray using a coded language unknown to the believer and the satanic ensemble but perfectly understood by God. Fourth, the Holy Spirit decodes the believer's prayer and packages it in a way that is acceptable to Father God.

> O the depth of the riches both of the wisdom and knowledge of God! How unsearchable are His judgments, and His ways past finding out! (Rom. 11:33 KJV)

```
         ┌──────────────────┐
         │  The Holy Spirit │
         │    Nudges the    │
         │  Believer to Pray│
         └──────────────────┘
        ↗                    ↘
┌──────────────┐       ┌──────────────┐
│  Father God  │       │ The Believer │
│  Answers the │       │   Prays in a │
│Believer's Pr.│       │Coded Language│
└──────────────┘       └──────────────┘
        ↖                    ↙
         ┌──────────────────┐
         │  The Holy Spirit │
         │    Decodes the   │
         │ Believer's Prayer│
         └──────────────────┘
```

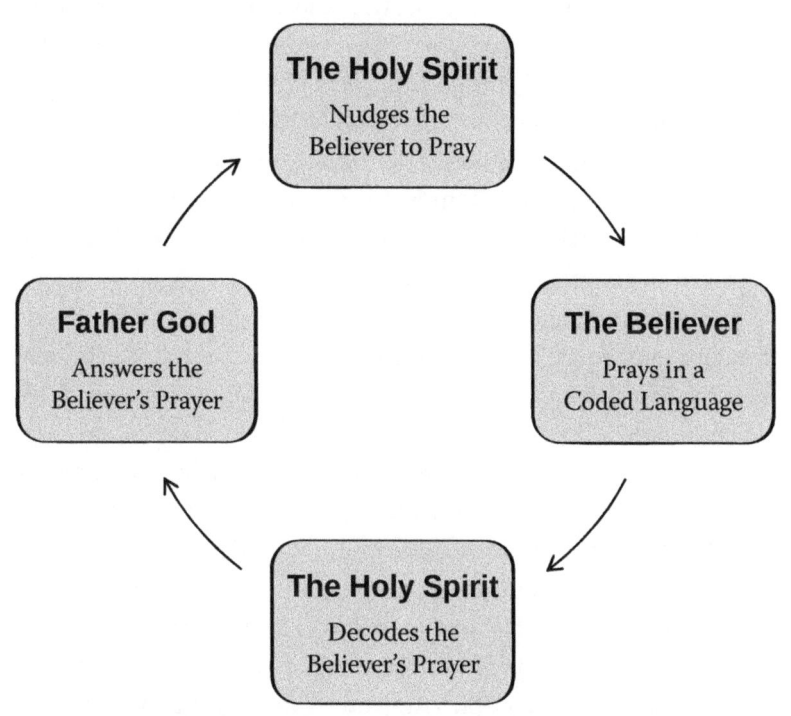

*Figure 2: How the Holy Spirit Helps the Believer Pray*

## VI: Floodgate to the Supernatural

Based on firsthand experience and scriptural examples, I can infer that the baptism in the Holy Spirit opens the floodgates to the supernatural. I have seen timid and even cynical believers (including me) totally transformed and begin to operate in the realm of the supernatural once they received the baptism in the Holy Spirit. Right now, in our churches in Worcester and Leominster, Massachusetts, we are blessed with a group of young adults who are on fire for the Lord and are championing the cause of Christ. It all began after they received the baptism in the Holy Spirit!

I will never forget how God totally transformed a friend of mine, Mike, from a regular guy to a dynamic young man with incredible manifestations of power and seamless access to the supernatural. It all began when Mike received the baptism in the Holy Spirit at a youth camp. Mike was gone for only a week, but he returned from the youth camp completely changed. He came back with "fire in his bones." The floodgates to the supernatural were literally opened to him as he began to manifest incredible supernatural giftings we had never seen him exercise before he received the baptism in the Holy Spirit.

At our prayer meetings, Mike began to prophesy and interpret tongues spoken by others. Mike's prophesies were powerful and spectacular. Though skinny like me, when Mike prophesied, his voice sounded like thunder, and he walked up and down the aisles with his eyes closed but he never collided with anyone or anything. It was an amazing sight considering the fact that our meetings were held in a middle school classroom with desks, tables, chairs, and bookshelves—not to mention our musical instruments.

Mike also began to operate in several other gifts of the Holy Spirit, including word of knowledge and discerning of spirits. His sensitivity to the Holy Spirit was awesome. On many occasions when we were walking on the street, he could identify people who had demonic spirits. Apparently, they could also recognize the enormous power Mike carried because they often sneaked away before Mike could confront them.

During the formative stages of our ministry in the 1980s, we used to pray for the Lord to guide us to know who should serve in the various departments of the ministry. The Holy Spirit used Mike to give us special revelations and divine guidance just as it

*The Holy Spirit*

happened in the Acts of the Apostles. For example, while praying for the Lord to show us those who should serve in the counseling, prayer, and outreach departments, the Holy Spirit used Mike to mention the names of those the Lord had ordained to serve in those departments. On one such occasion, he mentioned my name in full. After the meeting, he came to me and asked, "Is your middle name Acheampong?" Under the inspiration of the Holy Spirit, he had mentioned my full name without his prior knowledge. It was simply amazing!

## New Testament Examples

The New Testament believers began to operate in the supernatural after they had been baptized in the Holy Spirit. They became unstoppable in spreading the Gospel, they cast out demons, and the Lord worked with them daily attesting to their words and works. Peter and Paul were classic examples of New Testament believers who operated in the supernatural realm after receiving infusion of power from the resurrected Christ.

Peter used to be fearful and was initially hesitant to obey the Lord's order to go to the entire world and preach the Gospel. However, after he was baptized in the Holy Spirit on the Day of Pentecost, he received new boldness and led the first-century Church to turn the world upside down for Jesus. The following are some of the memorable feats Peter performed through the power of the Holy Spirit:

- healing of the lame man in Jerusalem (Acts 3:1–13)
- raising of Dorcas from death to life at Joppa (Acts 9:36–41)
- striking Elymas with blindness at Paphos (Acts 13:6–11)

Paul was a zealous persecutor of the Church, but when he received a life-changing encounter with the resurrected Christ and was subsequently filled with the Holy Spirit, he received new orders from the Lord Jesus to be an apostle to the Gentiles (Acts 9:15–17;

Romans 11:13). The following are some of Paul's outstanding supernatural feats recorded in scripture:

- healing of a cripple at Lystra (Acts 14:8–10)
- casting out the spirit of divination from a maid in Philippi (Acts 16:16–18)
- administering the baptism in the Holy Spirit at Ephesus (Acts 19:1–6)
- performing extraordinary miracles at Ephesus (Acts 19:11–12)
- restoring Eutychus to life at Troas (Acts 20:9–12)

**How to Receive the Baptism in the Holy Spirit**

The Bible clearly provides a pattern by which any believer in Christ can receive the baptism in the Holy Spirit with the evidence of speaking in tongues. It can happen either by the laying on of hands of another believer who has already received the baptism or by receiving it directly from the Lord Jesus Himself in your private prayer or during corporate prayer. In all these cases, you will have to submit to the following pattern:

**I: Recognize Your Need**

Like everything else God gives, it begins with us recognizing our personal need for the gift. Jesus calls this recognition of need "being thirsty."

> On the last and greatest day of the festival, Jesus stood and said in a loud voice, "*Let anyone who is thirsty come to me and drink.* Whoever believes in me, as scripture has said, rivers of living water will flow from within them." By this he meant the Spirit, whom those who believed in him were later to receive. Up to that time the Spirit had not been

given, since Jesus had not yet been glorified. (John 7:37–39 NIV, emphasis mine)

Undoubtedly, thirst is one of the most intense of human needs. A thirsty person would do anything to quench their thirst. This is the attitude Jesus wants us to have when we come to Him for the Holy Spirit. He wants us to be "thirsty." Jesus wants you to desire the Holy Spirit with such desperation as if your very life depends on it. To those who are thirsty for the living streams of the Holy Spirit, the Lord Jesus invites you to come to Him and drink. Lack of spiritual thirst is one of the several reasons why people don't receive the baptism in the Holy Spirit.

> **Remember**
>
> *Lack of spiritual thirst is one of the several reasons why people don't receive the baptism in the Holy Spirit.*

This first step is crucial for receiving anything from God. God usually does not give to us something we don't think we need. I have been intentional in sharing with you examples from the Bible and my own experiences to help you recognize that the baptism in the Holy Spirit is part of God's package, which is designed to make you effective in your Christian living and ministry.

About five years ago, while teaching on the baptism of the Holy Spirit to a group of intercessors, a fine elderly woman with an Episcopal background asked me whether one can be a successful Christian without receiving the baptism in the Holy Spirit. I told her a little bit about my pendulum experience and explained that I know of many believers (including ministers of the Gospel) who have not received the baptism in the Holy Spirit. That does not make them any less Christian. However, I certainly want everything God has provided for me. On hearing this explanation, she walked up to me to have me pray for her. I stopped teaching and laid hands on her, and she immediately burst out speaking in a clear unknown language. Looking at another woman, I discerned that she was ready to receive the baptism, so I called her forward. Before I could lay hands on her, she also burst out in tongues, praising the Lord.

So, if you want to receive the baptism in the Holy Spirit, the first step is acknowledging your need for it. You must have a desperate desire and need to be filled with the Holy Spirit. It requires humility and willingness to receive the grace gift you need to fulfill God's purpose for your life.

## II: Empty Your Vessel

The Holy Spirit can only fill a vessel that is empty and clean (2 Tim. 2:21). Because He is holy, you must cleanse yourself from anything that is incompatible with the nature and character of the Holy Spirit.

> Therefore, if anyone cleanses himself from what is dishonorable, he will be a vessel for honorable use, set apart as holy, useful to the master of the house, ready for every good work. (2 Tim. 2:21 ESV)

If you are filled with what A. W. Tozer calls "self sins" (such as self-confidence, self-reliance, selfishness, self-righteousness, etc.), the Holy Spirit cannot have room in you. You must rid yourself of every known sin and weight and ask God to cleanse you thoroughly with the blood of Jesus (Heb. 12:2; 1 John 1:9). You must also abdicate your will to the Holy Spirit and be willing to let Him have His own way in you. In other words, you must surrender your life totally to the Holy Spirit—for His exclusive use. Be ready to crown Him Lord of your life.

## III: Ask God for the Blessing

The third step is to ask God to baptize you in the Holy Spirit. In Luke 11:13, Jesus says, "Your loving, heavenly Father *will* give the Holy Spirit to those who *ask* Him." The responsibility for receiving the Holy Spirit, therefore, is not on God but on you. Many Christians have not received the baptism in the Holy Spirit because they have not asked God for it. There are also those who think "If God wants me to receive it, He will give it to me anyway." Well, God *wants* you to receive His blessing, but *you have to ask* for it.

> If ye then, being evil, know how to give good gifts unto your children: how much more shall your heavenly Father give the Holy Spirit *to them that ask him*? (Luke 11:13 KJV, emphasis mine)

> *Ask and it will be given to you*; seek and you will find; knock and the door will be opened to you. *For everyone who asks receives*; the one who seeks finds; and to the one who knocks, the door will be opened. (Matt 7:7–8 NIV, emphasis mine)

## IV: Receive by Faith

Christianity is a life of faith. We are born again by believing in the finished work of Christ on the cross and confessing Jesus Christ as Lord, we receive healing by faith in God's promises, and we receive answers to our prayers by faith in the written Word of God. Similarly, we receive the Holy Spirit by faith. After asking God to baptize you in the Holy Spirit, you must exercise your faith by speaking out the words the Holy Spirit puts in your mouth.

Jesus says, "Whatever you ask for in prayer, believe that you have received it, and it will be yours" (Mark 11:24 NIV). This means if you ask the Father for the Holy Spirit, you must believe that you have received the Holy Spirit. By faith, "drink" the living waters of the Holy Spirit. As the Holy Spirit fills you to overflow, He will express Himself by giving you words of praise to God in a language unknown to you. By faith, release the streams of living water from your innermost being. Let go your understanding. Let the Holy Spirit take over. Swim in the living streams of the Holy Spirit. Go ahead and pray in tongues. Your spirit will be praying, but your mind will not understand what you are saying (1 Cor. 14:14). Just go ahead and worship God in your new supernatural language. Hallelujah!

**Chapter Takeaway**

It is not enough to be born again. God wants to infuse you with His power.

- The baptism in the Holy Spirit infuses you with power to testify about Christ.
- The baptism in the Holy Spirit is called different terms in the Bible.
- The promise of the Holy Spirit is for every born-again believer in Christ.
- God is pouring out His Spirit on people from all manner of backgrounds.
- If you are thirsty and willing, you can receive the gift of the Holy Spirit.
- I have experienced the Holy Spirit as my indispensable friend—have you?

**Chapter Challenge**

If you have not received the baptism in the Holy Spirit but are desirous to do so, would you set some time aside this week to ask Jesus to baptize you?

- If you have already received the baptism in the Holy Spirit, would you ask the Holy Spirit to lead you to someone who needs the Spirit's infusion of power? When the Holy Spirit

leads you to the person, I will challenge to share what you have learned from this chapter and pray for the person to receive the baptism in the Holy Spirit.
- What is the Lord doing in your life?

# Chapter 9

## Indispensable for End-Time Ministry

*The end-time Church cannot do by the flesh what the early Church accomplished by the Spirit. Since the Church was born by the power of the Holy Spirit, it must end by the same. The Church was inaugurated in power; in power must it continue till it is raptured into glory!*

ON GOD'S PROPHETIC CALENDAR, we are living in the end-time. According to Bible prophecy, the end-time will be characterized by unimaginable vices such as increased wickedness (2 Tim. 3:13), widespread depravity and godlessness (Luke 17:26–27), and increased occult activities (2 Tim. 3:7–8, 13). The end-time will also be marked by extreme self-love and love for pleasure (2 Tim. 3:1–5), worldwide persecution of Christians, increased emergence of false prophets and teachers, and an increase in natural disasters, terrorism, and armed conflicts and wars (Matt. 24:4–13). Any objective observer of contemporary global events will agree that all these prophecies are being fulfilled before our very eyes. We can, therefore, agree with God that we are indeed living in the last days.

Knowing that his time is almost up, Satan is filled with fury and is unleashing his worst arsenals against the people of God (Rev. 12:12). Being fully aware that his destination is the Lake of Fire and desperate to frustrate the purposes of God, Satan is unleashing multiple tricks and attacks on humanity, including self-believism (as opposed to belief in God alone), Eastern religious beliefs rebranded as motivational messages, and the lie that all faiths lead to God. If ever there was a time when the people of God needed to be fully armed with all the resources of God to overcome the cunning strategies of Satan, it is now. Our adversary is fierce, and the battle is intense, but the "weapons we fight with are not the weapons of the world. On the contrary, they have divine power to demolish strongholds" (2 Cor. 10:4 NIV).

The end-time is not all gloomy, though. The power of the Holy Spirit residing in us as Christians can overthrow any and every satanic strategy and power. As our indispensable Helper for getting the end-time ministry done, the Holy Spirit works through us to regenerate lost souls, facilitate our spiritual growth, equip us for ministry, and prepare us for the Lord's return. God has reserved His best for the last days. He has ordained a worldwide outpouring of the Holy Spirit (aided by advanced technology) to accelerate worldwide preaching of the Gospel.

The knowledge of the glory of the Lord is filling the earth as the waters cover the sea (Hab. 2:14). The Holy Spirit is stirring up young people all over the world to offer up worship and praise to God in stadiums, parks, and other public places. He is simultaneously pouring out the former and latter rains of the Holy Spirit on His people (Joel 2:28–29; Matt. 24:14; Hab. 2:14).

In the rest of this chapter, we shall discuss the role of the Holy Spirit in the contemporary Church as our indispensable partner for end-time ministry. We will approach it from two different perspectives. First, we will examine the work of the Holy Spirit in the Church for effective end-time ministry. Secondly, we will discuss the indispensable role of the Holy Spirit in the life of the individual believer.

## Role of the Holy Spirit in the End-Time Church

The indispensable role of the Holy Spirit in the Church for end-time ministry cannot be overemphasized. From the Lord's command to His disciples not to begin ministry until they were endued with power to the transformational role of the Holy Spirit throughout Church history, the indispensability of the Holy Spirit in the church is well attested. In the Church, the Holy Spirit is Lord and exalts Christ as Lord over His Body. The Holy Spirit empowers Church leaders and anoints them with wisdom, knowledge, understanding, and insight to lead the flock. Together with the infallible Word, the Holy Spirit sanctifies and cleanses the Lord's bride, and will present her holy and without blemish to the Lord on His return (Eph. 5:26–27).

Two major ways by which the Holy Spirit works in the Church today are through God's delegated representatives and through the use of spiritual gifts exercised by ordinary believers. For the Church to function as Christ ordained it, there must be full operation of all fivefold ministries, all seven gifts from Father God (Rom. 12:4–8), and all three categories of the gifts of the Spirit. I will throw more light on this shortly.

Meanwhile, please don't let anyone deceive you into believing that some of the ministry gifts or spiritual gifts have ceased. By implication, those who teach these things claim that the Church does not need some or all the gifts of the Spirit anymore. The amazing thing is that those who deny the operation of spiritual gifts are quick to brand people as false teachers and prophets. In other words, they believe in the existence of counterfeit gifts and satanic powers working through men. The obvious question is, How can there be a counterfeit without the genuine?

> **Remember**
>
> *The capacity of the Holy Spirit to do with today's church what He did through the first-century church remains unchanged.*

The capacity of the Holy Spirit to do with today's Church what He did through the first-century Church remains unchanged. All over the world, the Holy Spirit continues to do what we read about in the New Testament. He is eager to give His gifts and manifest God's glory in any Church that would allow Him to be Lord. The only people who cannot live out the New Testament experience are those who believe and teach that the gifts and power of the Holy Spirit as recorded in the New Testament have ceased. Interestingly, when they see the manifestation of the Holy Spirit right in their faces, they still have a theological explanation (which are inconsistent with the spirit of scripture) to explain the undeniable.

As far as I am concerned, there is nothing better in life than to identify what God is doing and to be part of it. Scripture is clear. The Lord Jesus is alive today and is actively working out His supernatural end-time purposes through and in partnership with any individual and group of believers who are willing to be used of His Spirit.

If ever there was a time when the Church needed the full operation of spiritual gifts and the ministry gifts, it is now! We need these supernatural gifts to sharpen the preaching of God's infallible Word. We need the ministry and spiritual gifts to defeat the fierce onslaughts of satanic powers, and we need ministry and spiritual gifts to rein in the end-time harvest of souls. In other words, we need the ministry and spiritual gifts to do the work of the ministry. If the early Church needed the ministry and spiritual gifts to break the fallow ground, then the latter Church cannot be expected to bring in the end-time harvest with less ministry and fewer spiritual gifts. It needs more.

## Indispensable Role of the Holy Spirit in Church Government

When our Lord Jesus ascended on high and sat at the right hand of the Father, He gave His Church human gifts called apostles, prophets, evangelists, pastors, and teachers (Eph. 4:11–13).

> Now these are the gifts Christ gave to the Church: the apostles, the prophets, the evangelists, and the pastors and teachers. Their responsibility is to equip God's people to do his work and build up the church, the body of Christ. *This will continue until we all come to such unity in our faith and knowledge of God's Son* that we will be mature in the Lord, measuring up to the full and complete standard of Christ. (Eph. 4:11–13 NLT, emphasis mine)

The risen Lord has given His Church the fivefold ministry gifts to equip God's people for the work of the ministry and to build up the body of Christ (the church). The Lord's threefold goal for giving the ministry gifts are to bring:

- the Church into the unity of the faith through the knowledge of Christ (Eph. 4:12)
- God's people to spiritual maturity (Eph. 4:13)
- the Church to a place its members could be true representation of Christ (Eph. 4:13).

With the exception of the pastoral ministry, the grace given to the fivefold ministers usually transcends the local church to the entire Church universal (Eph. 4:11). The responsibilities of the fivefold ministers include receiving divine revelations (Gal. 1:20–21; 2 Cor. 11:23; Eph. 3:3), building structures for the Church (Eph. 2:19–20), and developing and commissioning leaders (Acts 13:1–3). They build up believers to develop healthy interpersonal relations and attitudes, and they have the capacity to impart spiritual gifts through transfer of divine power and the prophetic Word (Rom. 1:11; 2 Tim. 1:6).

The scope of this book will not allow me to do a thorough discussion of the role of each of the fivefold ministry gifts. I will, therefore, make brief comments about each of the fivefold ministry.

## Apostles

Apostles are ministry pioneers, groundbreakers, church planters, or master builders. They are gifted with special supernatural grace for building structures for the Church (Eph. 2:19–20). Apostles are endowed with, at least, one revelation gift, one power gift, and one prophetic gift. Examples of New Testament apostles are Peter, John, Paul, Silas, and Barnabas.

## Prophets

Prophets speak forth God's Word by divine revelation. Together with apostles, prophets build structures for the Church (Eph. 2:19–20). They are endowed with, at least, two prophetic gifts and at least one revelational gift or two revelational gifts and one vocal gift. Examples of New Testament prophets are Agabus (Acts 11:27–30), Judas, and Silas (Acts 15:32).

## Evangelists

Evangelists proclaim the Gospel (good news) and lead sinners to the Savior. The ministry of the evangelist is typically accompanied by miraculous signs (Acts 8:6–7) and usually results in salvation followed by water baptism (Acts 8:12). Evangelists are endowed with at least one power gift and one vocal gift. Examples of New Testament evangelists are Philip (Acts 8:4–8; 26–40) and Stephen (Acts 6:8–10).

## Pastors or Shepherds

Pastors have spiritual oversight over the local assembly. They lead, nourish (feed), and protect the Lord's "flock." It is the responsibility of shepherds to appoint elders and deacons (Titus 1:5–9). Pastors have a "shepherd's heart" and are usually self-sacrificing for the "flock" (John 10:1–28). Among other responsibilities, pastors use scriptures to develop doctrine (Acts 15:22–29), settle disputes

(Matt. 18:17), and regulate moral conduct (1 Cor. 5:1–5; 6:1–2). They are endowed with the gifts of compassion, leadership, and teaching. Examples of New Testament pastors are Timothy (Acts 8:4–8; 26–40), Titus (Titus 1:5), and Peter (1 Pet. 5:1–4).

## Teachers

Teachers are interpreters and expositors of scriptures. They minister both to the universal Church (Eph. 4:11) as well as the local church (1 Tim. 5:17). Teachers may be endowed with a variety of the spiritual gifts. The ministry of the teacher results in clarity and understanding of scripture and spiritual maturity (Acts 20:20–21). Examples of New Testament teachers are Paul (2 Tim. 1:11), Apollos (Acts 18:24–28; 1 Cor. 3:5–6), and Barnabas (Acts 13:1–4).

## Multiplicity of Offices

People who are called to the fivefold ministry usually function in more than one office. For example, Paul was an apostle, prophet, and a teacher (Acts 13:1–4; 2 Tim. 1:11); Barnabas was an apostle, a prophet, and a teacher; Timothy was an apostle, pastor, and an evangelist (1 Thess. 1:1; Acts 19:22; 1 Tim. 4:11; 2 Tim. 4:5); and Jesus was an apostle (Heb. 3:1), a teacher (Luke 20:1; John 3:1–2), an evangelist (John 4:34–35), a shepherd (John 10:11), and a prophet (Acts 7:37).

The Holy Spirit works through the fivefold ministry to exercise governmental authority in the Church. Indeed, one of the main reasons why the Lord ordained governmental leadership (apostles, prophets, evangelists, pastors, and teachers) is to set the church in order. That means, these leaders have been given the authority to ensure that the body of Christ operates as the Head (Christ) directs and decides. The Lord Jesus rules in His Church by the Holy Spirit through His human delegated leaders (five-fold ministers). So, when the church meets, the leaders must be sensitive to the leading of the Holy Spirit and be able to discern what the Spirit might be saying, doing, or signaling. I will illustrate with an example.

At a camp meeting in September 1984, the manifest presence of the Holy Spirit became tangible in the auditorium as I led the people of God in worship. People were being slain in the spirit, some prostrated on the floor in worship, and others sang and laughed in the spirit. After a while, the auditorium became quiet. The Lord gave me a prophetic word to encourage His people, but I hesitated to speak forth because I was afraid of the "big men" (guest speakers) sitting in the front row (I was nineteen years old). Just then, the main guest speaker intervened and said, "Well, Brother Emmanuel, the Lord has given you a word for His people." Relieved, I boldly spoke the prophecy (word of encouragement) the Lord had given me.

The guest speaker's action illustrates the role governmental leaders are expected to play during corporate meetings. They are expected to discern the moves of the Spirit during church services and ensure proper functioning of the gifts of the Spirit through example and teaching. In order words, the fivefold ministers must set guidelines for the proper use of the gifts of the Holy Spirit, ensure order in the church, and avoid confusion. The goal is to lift up the name of Lord Jesus.

If the Church lacks the full operation of the fivefold ministry, the body of Christ would be malnourished, spiritually immature, gullible, and highly unstable (Eph. 4:14). The Lord's Church will not attain the full supply of spiritual nourishment and impartation of power if it lacks any one of the fivefold ministry. Heads of local assemblies and/or denominations who, for whatever reason, do not expose their members to all fivefold ministries are doing their flocks a great disservice. Denial of the full

> **Remember**
>
> *If the Church lacks the full operation of the fivefold ministry, the body of Christ would be malnourished, spiritually immature, gullible, and highly unstable (Eph. 4:14).*

operation of the ministry gifts is perhaps the main reason why a large proportion of the Church is increasingly becoming spiritually immature and highly susceptible to the deceitful craftiness of false teachers, prophets, and manipulators (Eph. 4:14).

Let me close the discussion on the fivefold ministry gifts by noting that the Bible says the responsibility of the fivefold ministry gifts will continue until we all come to such unity in our faith and knowledge of God's Son that we will be mature in the Lord, measuring up to the full and complete standard of Christ (Eph. 4:13 NLT). Since the church has not achieved the objectives stated above, it is reasonable to expect all five ministry gifts to continue to function. Indeed, the Church will need the ministry gifts till the Lord Jesus returns for His bride, the church.

## Indispensable Role of the Holy Spirit in Church Worship

The second major means by which the Holy Spirit is using the end-time church to fulfill God's agenda is through the operation of spiritual gifts exercised through believers in Christ—irrespective of educational level, racial background, or socioeconomic status. The exercise of supernatural gifts also allows the Church to enforce the victory Jesus won for us by His Crucifixion, death, and resurrection. Through the use of spiritual gifts, people can experience life-changing encounters with the risen Lord, those who are being oppressed by incurable diseases can receive their healing, and those who are bound by oppressive satanic forces can be set free.

> If an unbeliever or an inquirer comes in while everyone is prophesying, they are convicted of sin and are brought under judgment by all, as the secrets of their hearts are laid bare. So they will fall down and worship God, exclaiming, "God is really among you!" (1 Cor. 14:24–25 NIV)

## The Gifts of the Holy Spirit

The Bible teaches that the Holy Spirit gives spiritual gifts to all believers (1 Peter 4:10 – 11; Rom. 12:4 – 8). Every believer is given at least one spiritual gift for the general good of the entire church. Thus, we can say the gifts are given to the church, but they operate through individual believers.

> But the manifestation of the Spirit is given to every man to profit withal. For to one is given by the Spirit the word of wisdom; to another the word of knowledge by the same Spirit; To another faith by the same Spirit; to another the gifts of healing by the same Spirit; To another the working of miracles; to another prophecy; to another discerning of spirits; to another divers kinds of tongues; to another the interpretation of tongues: But all these worketh that one and the selfsame Spirit, dividing to every man severally as he will. (1 Cor. 12:7–11 KJV)

Nine spiritual gifts are explicitly mentioned in the above scripture. These nine gifts of the Spirit are usually put into three categories: revelation gifts (gifts of vision), power gifts, and prophetic gifts (vocal gifts) as shown below:

| Revelation Gifts | Power Gifts | Vocal (Prophetic) Gifts |
| --- | --- | --- |
| Word of wisdom | Gift of faith | Prophecy |
| Word of knowledge | Gifts of healings | Diverse kinds of tongues |
| Discerning of spirits | Working of miracles | Interpretation of tongues |

## Nature of the Gifts of the Spirit

The gifts of the Holy Spirit are gifts of grace and thus cannot be earned. They are freely distributed to believers according to the will of the Holy Spirit. Thus, the kind of gift you receive from the Holy Spirit does not depend on your educational level, socioeconomic status, or even spiritual maturity. It is the prerogative of the Holy Spirit to distribute the gifts as He wishes.

I know of Christians across the educational and social spectrum who have been blessed with the same spiritual gifts. I have seen engineers, medical doctors, and lawyers being used by the Holy Spirit in the areas of healing, prophecy, and working of miracles. I also know of people with very little education being used of God in all three categories of gifts of the Holy Spirit, including word of knowledge, word of wisdom, discerning of spirits, prophecy, and working of miracles. Despite their varied backgrounds, the spiritual power, revelation, and prophetic utterances these believers exercise come from one source: the Holy Spirit. It has very little to do with educational, geographical, or socioeconomic background.

Next, the gifts of the Spirit are supernatural in nature. Therefore, they cannot be obtained through human effort or explained by natural intellect, human insight, or human skill. Spiritual gifts defy natural explanation. For example, we cannot apply medical science to explain how a person suffering from a brain tumor is healed after someone with a gift of healing prays for them. Neither can we use the laws of psychiatry to explain how a person suffering from schizophrenia is instantly healed after prayer and the laying on of hands.

Again, though we stated that spiritual gifts are given as the Holy Spirit wishes, the Bible, however, urges us to "covet earnestly the best gifts" (1 Cor. 12:31 KJV). This suggests that the Holy Spirit will give us gifts we desire.

> Let love be your highest goal! But you should also *desire the special abilities the Spirit gives*—especially the ability to prophesy. (1 Cor. 14:1 NLT, emphasis mine)

I can attest to this in my personal life and ministry. When I perceive the need for the operation of a particular spiritual gift and begin to pray about it, I tend to develop a strong desire for it. When I open up to the Holy Spirit, He gives me that gift to bless the people of God. I typically say, "Holy Spirit, if you want someone to use to speak to your people, I am available" or "Holy Spirit, if you want someone to use in the exercise of discerning of spirits, I am here. You may use me." When I make myself available, He normally gives me the ability to operate in that gift. I believe it is the Holy Spirit who makes me sense the need and helps me desire to be used. So, He gets all the credit.

The gifts of the Spirit can also be misused and even abused. In fact, Paul's discourse of the gifts of the Spirit in 1 Corinthians chapters 12 and 14 was prompted by the misuse of the gifts of the Spirit in the church in Corinth. Though the Corinthian church was blessed with spiritual gifts, it was spiritually immature as evidenced by the works of the flesh they manifested such as episodes of quarrelling, dissensions, strife, jealousy (1 Cor. 3:1–4), immorality (1 Cor. 5:1–2), and abuse of the Lord's table (1 Cor. 11:17–22). Much of Paul's epistle to the Corinthian church was devoted to addressing misuse of God's gifts of grace, including the gifts of the Holy Spirit.

## Purpose of Spiritual Gifts

I believe the Holy Spirit gives us spiritual gifts for three main reasons. First, the gifts of the Holy Spirit are given for the edification of the entire body of Christ. "Now to each one the manifestation of the Spirit is given *for the common good*" (1 Cor. 12:7 NIV, emphasis mine). The gifts of the Holy Spirit are not the personal property of individual believers. They are given for the general benefit of the body of Christ. They are not personal trophies; they are tools given to profit the church.

Many years ago, the leader of a Christian fellowship I belonged to offended a brother who was highly gifted in the areas of word of knowledge, prophecy, and discerning of spirits. In retaliation, the offended brother decided to skip a very important program where he knew his gifts would be needed. To our pleasant surprise, the Holy Spirit showed up that day and used another person who had never prophesied before to bless the group. The lesson is clear. If you think you can hoard or monopolize your spiritual gift(s), the Holy Spirit will use someone else to bless His church.

Second, the gifts of the Holy Spirit are given to us so we can glorify God. God's purpose for every gift He gives us is to bring glory to His name. Our chief calling is to glorify God in everything we do. "So whether you eat or drink or whatever you do, do it all for the glory of God" (1 Cor.10:31 NIV).

> If anyone speaks, he should speak as one conveying the words of God. If anyone serves, he should serve with the strength God supplies, so that in all things God may be glorified through Jesus Christ, to whom be the glory and the power forever and ever. Amen. (1 Pet. 4:11 Berean Study Bible)

Third, when we exercise the gifts of the Spirit, we bring in the open the superiority of God's kingdom over Satan's kingdom. This is especially true when we exercise the revelational and power gifts. The revelational gifts reveal God's prophetic purposes for His church as well as bring in the open Satan's hidden agenda and operations, while the power gifts are used to demolish hidden satanic oppression and yokes. The exercise of spiritual gifts forces satanic agents to admit that "this is the finger of God" (Exo. 8:19 NIV), and that brings glory to God. When Jesus was accused of healing and casting out demons by satanic power, He replied, "If I drive out demons by the finger of God, then the kingdom of God has come upon you" (Luke 11:20 NIV). Thus, exercising spiritual gifts such as healing and casting out demons brings glory to God because it is a sign that the kingdom of God is among His people.

**How Can We Receive Spiritual Gifts?**

Understand that God has given you, at least, one spiritual gift:

> Now to each one the manifestation of the Spirit *is given* for the common good. (1 Cor. 12:7 NIV, emphasis mine)

The scripture is clear: God has given every believer a gift for the benefit of the entire Body of Christ and to the glory of God. This means failing to use our gifts deprives the Church a spiritual blessing God wants it to experience and God does not receive the glorify due Him by our use of spiritual gifts. The burden is on us as believers to discover our spiritual gifts and put them into use. If you don't know the gifts the Holy Spirit has given you, you must ask Him to reveal them to you. In your prayer, if you desire a particular gift, and your motive for that desire is pure, you must tell the Holy Spirit you desire that particular gift.

> For the LORD God is a sun and shield; the LORD bestows favor and honor. *No good thing does he withhold from those who walk uprightly.* (Ps. 84:11 ESV, emphasis mine)

If you want to discover your spiritual gifts, the first thing you must do is develop the attitude of humility. God gives His gifts to the humble (James 4:6). You can't receive anything from God if your heart is haughty and you want to use the gift to show off. Your motives must be right and pure. Because the human heart is deceitful, it is important to ask the Lord to examine the motives of your heart (Prov. 16:2). If He reveals any impurity, ask Him to cleanse you and make you pure within.

Next, understand that you must receive spiritual gifts by faith. Like salvation, spiritual gifts are gifts of grace—and grace comes through faith (Eph. 2:8). You can't work for them. If the invisible Holy Spirit regularly manifests Himself outwardly through you in terms of a particular gift, then that is your spiritual gift. In other words, you will know you have a particular spiritual gift if that gift manifests in your life regularly. For example, if people receive their healing whenever you pray over them, then the Holy Spirit has given the gift of healing. If you are regularly given the interpretation to messages spoken in tongues, then you have been given the gift of interpretation of tongues.

Finally, the baptism in the Holy Spirit opens the floodgate to spiritual gifts. Both in the recorded account of scripture and from personal walk with God, it is clear that when people receive the baptism in the Holy Spirit with the evidence of speaking in tongues; they begin to manifest the gifts of the Holy Spirit. That means the surest route to receiving the gifts of the Holy Spirit is to receive the baptism in the Holy Spirit as described in chapter 8 of this book. In other words, the baptism in the Holy Spirit is a shortcut to the gifts of the Holy Spirit. It's a package. When you receive the baptism in the Holy Spirit, you open the floodgate to the supernatural, which includes the gifts of the Holy Spirit. This is another reason God wants all His children to receive the baptism in the Holy Spirit as described in chapter 8.

## Revelation Gifts

The revelation gifts refer to the supernatural ability to receive information about a person or situation that one could not have received by one's own learning. There are different ways by which the believer may receive the supernatural revelation. Sometimes it may come in the form of a vision, where natural events appear to be suspended and the believer sees what the Holy Spirit wants His people to know. At other times, it comes as a strong perception or a deep "knowing" in your spirit. The revelation gifts comprise word of wisdom, word of knowledge, and discerning of spirits.

## Word of Wisdom

The gift of the word of wisdom is a chip of God's infinite wisdom concerning the prophetic destiny of the Church, a local church, or an individual believer. A person operating this gift speaks into the future of a situation or person by a direct revelation of the Holy Spirit. The gift of word of wisdom is different from natural wisdom or "educated" wisdom acquired through "wisdom studies" such as psychology, astrology, or psychiatry.

## Examples of Word of Wisdom from the Bible

There are many examples of word of wisdom in the Bible. All the prophets who foretold future events, including the first coming of Christ, Israel's exile and return to the promised land, and outpouring of the Holy Spirit, operated by the gift of word of wisdom. In the New Testament, both our Lord Jesus Christ and the apostles operated in the gift of word of wisdom. Here are some examples:

> Jesus said to Peter, "Go down to the lake and throw in a line. Open the mouth of the first fish you catch, and you will find a large silver coin. Take it and pay the tax for both of us." (Matt. 17:27 NLT)

How did Jesus know this? He knew it through the word of wisdom.

> When he had finished speaking, he said to Simon, "Put out into deep water, and let down the nets for a catch." When they had done so, they caught such a large number of fish that their nets began to break. (Luke 5:4–6 NIV)

The apostle James spoke the mind of God by the word of wisdom at the Jerusalem Council. When he was done speaking, the church leaders knew that the matter was settled and the contention was over. (Acts 15:13–20)

## Examples from My Life

Since my conversion at age twelve, I have had the privileged of witnessing the operation of the word of wisdom at close range. I have had the blessing of being exposed to the awesome revelation ministries of men like Brother Bhekie (see chapter 12), my friend Mike, and many otherwise regular guys who were great men of God. Over the years, I have had powerful impartation of spiritual gifts through the laying on of hands of anointed men of God. Through the ministry of Brother Bhekie (mainly), I have been blessed with the gift of word of wisdom. Therefore, I have firsthand experience, knowledge, and understanding about how the gift of word of wisdom works. A few examples will suffice.

Around Christmastime 2014, Sister Phyllis—my prayer partner and a godly woman—took me to see her daughter and grandchildren in Decatur, Georgia. As soon as I saw her youngest grandson, the Holy Spirit revealed to me the young boy's future. I gave him a hug and told him that the hand of God was upon him—and that the Lord was going to use him in a miraculous way. Humanly speaking, I knew nothing about this fifteen-year-old boy. Later, during our prayer sessions, Sister Phyllis would ask me to pray for the salvation of this grandson and for him to withstand bad influence.

About two years later, Sister Phyllis called me and told me that her grandson had been born again about a year ago and that the Lord was using him powerfully in evangelizing his peers. Then she said, "My grandson has been asking of you because he remembers the prophetic word you spoke over His life." All I could say was "All the glory belongs to God."

A couple of years ago, a group of young adults in our Worcester church asked me to pray with them. As I laid hands on them to pray, the Holy Spirit began to reveal their prophetic future to me. I followed the leading of the Spirit and spoke over each of them concerning what the Holy Spirit was showing to me. About seven months later, one of them asked me if I remembered the word of wisdom I pronounced over his life that day. Of course, I did. I had told him that the Lord was going to give him accelerated promotion. He informed me that shortly after I spoke over his life, he was promoted twice in the course of a few months and was now on par with his hiring manager. Hallelujah! But for the revelation of the Holy Spirit, there was no way I could know this.

## Word of Knowledge

The gift of word of knowledge is the supernatural ability to know something about a person or situation only because the Holy Spirit revealed it to you. It is the impartation of an infinitesimal amount of God's infinite knowledge to a believer for the benefit of the body of Christ. It always pertains to a specific existing fact and is thus devoid of any shade of ambiguity. Again, it is important to stress that the operation of this gift is not necessarily based on one's in-depth knowledge of scripture or theology, though these are useful. It comes as a momentary supernatural revelation from the Holy Spirit to the believer for the benefit of the entire church. Like all spiritual gifts, the source of this gift is the Holy Spirit, and its operation is miraculous and supernatural. I will give you examples both from the first-century church and from my own life's experience.

## Examples of Word of Knowledge from the Bible

- The Spirit told Peter, "Simon, three men are looking for you." (Acts 10:19)

- The Spirit said to Philip, "Go over to that chariot and stay by it." (Acts 8:29)
- The Holy spirit said, "Set apart for me Barnabas and Saul." (Acts 13:2)
- The Holy Spirit revealed the deceit of Ananias to Peter. (Acts 5:3)

## Examples from My Life

At the start of my final year in college, a dear Christian brother informed me that the leading soloist in their town had just arrived on campus as a freshman. He also told me that despite the young woman's exceptional gift, she had resolved not to join any campus group so she could concentrate on her studies.

Two days later, on my way to a lecture, I saw a young woman walking toward me. Suddenly, the Holy Spirit told me, "That's Vida, the lady Yaw told you about." I smiled at her and said, "You're Vida, aren't you?" Astonished, she replied, "Yes. How did you know my name—and who are you?" I explained how the Holy Spirit had revealed to me who she was and that the Lord would take her places if she would put His interest ahead of hers. I found myself prophesying to her and encouraging her to trust God with her gifts, time, and studies.

The combined operation of the gift of word of knowledge and prophecy convinced her about how much God knew and cared about her. Having received this life-transforming experience, Vida committed herself to the university's Christian music group of which I was the president. She was mightily used by God, and she excelled in her studies.

On another occasion, while we were making final preparations toward ministration in a certain church, the Holy Spirit revealed to my friend Mike that a certain woman with a contrary spirit would resist our ministry that morning. In the revelation, Mike gave an elaborate description of the woman: where she would sit, the color of her dress, and her skin color. We prayed and nullified this satanic orchestration.

When we entered the church, she was sitting right where Mike had predicted and looking exactly as Mike had described. Throughout the service, our prayer warriors who were meeting in a nearby house continued to fire spiritual arsenals against this satanic machination. The woman was apparently feeling the heat of the Holy Ghost because she kept fidgeting and sweating throughout the service; she left before Mike began his sermon. Thank God we did not experience any spiritual resistance, and about a third of the congregation responded to the invitation to receive Christ as their Lord and Savior.

## Discerning of Spirits

The gift of discerning of spirits is the supernatural ability to sense and distinguish between spirits. People with this gift typically have the supernatural ability to perceive the presence of different spirits in a meeting such as the sweet presence the Holy Spirit, the presence of a ministering angel, or the presence of evil spirits.

A believer with the gift of discerning of spirits can tell if a particular spirit is not of God, and can also identify the specific spirit(s) by name. Jesus exemplified this truth on many occasions when he identified and addressed specific demons in people. For example, in Matthew 9:32–33, the causative spirit in a deaf and dumb man was identified as a mute spirit. When Jesus cast out the mute spirit, the deaf and dumb man began to speak.

## Examples of the Gift of Discerning of Spirits from the Bible

There is an interesting example of how the gift of discerning of spirits operated in the apostle Paul. While evangelizing in the city of Philippi, a slave girl followed them daily declaring, "These men are the servants of the Most High God, who proclaim to us the way of salvation" (Acts 16:17 NKJV). Since the girl's testimony was true, many Christians would have been deceived into thinking she was operating by the Holy Spirit. Paul, however, knew by the gift of discerning of spirits that the spirit operating through the girl was not of God. After boldly identifying the spirit in the girl as the spirit of divination, Paul commanded the evil spirit to come out of her, and at that moment, the spirit left her (Acts 16:18 NIV).

In the city of Samaria, a sorcerer called Simon gained great fame by his supernatural powers and acts. Indeed, the people of Samaria believed Simon was "the Great Power of God" (Acts 8:10). However, when Philip came to the city and preached the Gospel with accompanying signs and miracles, the people believed the Gospel and received the Holy Spirit when the apostles Peter and John came from Jerusalem and laid their hands on them.

When Simon saw that the Spirit was given at the laying on of the apostles' hands, he offered them money and said, "Give me also this ability so that everyone on whom I lay my hands may receive the Holy Spirit" (Acts 8:8–9 NIV).

On hearing this, Peter sharply rebuked Simon for the wickedness of his heart and admonished him to ask God for forgiveness. Inspired by the Holy Spirit, Peter declared, "I see that you are full of bitterness and captive to sin" (Acts 8:23 NIV). Though Peter did not know Simon, he knew by the gift of discerning of spirits that Simon was not acting from mere greed or ignorance of spiritual things but from the evil spirit called sorcery.

### Examples from My Life

If ever there is a time when believers really need the gift of discerning of spirits, it is when we are dealing with evil spirits. Let me illustrate with just one example. A Christian sister invited a few of us to come over to her house to pray for their maidservant because "she was behaving weird." During the prayer, we stood in a circle with the maidservant in the center. As we prayed, she began to manifest the different demons operating in her. For example, she initially appeared indifferent as if to say, "What can you guys do?" and then suddenly, she became extremely angry and tried to storm out of the room. Immediately Mike said, "That's the spirit of rebellion and pride." With that revelation, we rebuked that spirit till she became calm and appeared normal. As we kept praying (mainly speaking in tongues), her countenance changed again. This time, she started laughing and taunting us. "We aren't going anywhere. We're here to stay."

Mike said, "That's the spirit of mockery." We launched into intensive spiritual warfare and cast out that spirit. Next, she began speaking French. That was strange because she had zero formal education, and the only language she could speak was her native dialect. We commanded the spirit to shut up and come out. She fell down and began to wiggle like a wounded snake.

Instantly, Mike identified the demon. "That's the spirit of subtlety and deception." We prayed and commanded that spirit to come out of her, and it did. Finally, she began to remove her clothes. Mike said, "That's the spirit of seduction."

We cast it out. When we were done casting out all the demons residing in her, she became calm and sober. We led her to pray the sinners' prayer and invite Jesus into her life. This time, when her countenance changed, she became radiant with the glory of the Lord. Glory to God!

**Power Gifts**

In one of the many coups d'état my country experienced when I was growing up, I witnessed a group of young military personnel bring down a three-story building with a relatively small amount of dynamite. The soldiers planted the dynamite at the foot of the building, and at the press of a button, the three-story house came crushing down. The miraculous power we receive from the Holy Spirit (Greek *dumamin*) has the same root meaning for English words such as dynamite and dynamic.

As the name suggests, the power gifts are dramatic in their

*The Holy Spirit*

outworking, sensational in their outcomes, and defying natural explanation. For example, it takes Holy Spirit-infused power to make a man born blind to see, heal a person with one leg shorter than the other in an instant, or raise a dead person back to life. Demonstration of such miraculous powers is made possible through the gifts of power.

When properly used, power gifts communicate God's omnipotence in a visible way and bring glory to God. The power gifts are a great blessing to the people who receive the miracles or healings these ministries bring. As indicated earlier, the gifts of power comprise the gift of faith, working of miracles, and the gifts of healings. Given the scope of this book, I cannot give a detailed description of each of these gifts and how they operate. I will, therefore, throw a brief light on how the power gifts work generally.

The gift of working of miracles is the supernatural ability to perform extraordinary feats by the power of the Holy Spirit. Examples of the operation of the gift of working of miracles in Jesus's ministry are turning water into wine (John 2:1–11), feeding of the five thousand (John 6:1–14), Jesus walking on the water (John 14:22–34), and the raising of Lazarus, who had been dead for four days (John 11:38–44). Examples of working of miracles in the early church include Peter raising Dorcas from the dead at Joppa (Acts 9:39–42), Paul raising Eutychus from the dead at Troas (Acts 20:8–12), Paul performing unspecified miracles at Iconium (Acts 14:3–4) and in Ephesus (Acts 19:11–12), and Paul shrugging off a viper at Malta (Acts 28:3–6).

The expression "gifts of healings" suggests there are diverse kinds of healing for different diseases. For instance, in the New Testament, people received their healing by many different means. Some were healed by the laying on of hands (Luke 13:13; 4:40; Mark 6:5; Acts 19:12, 17; 28:8). Some were healed by the spoken word (Acts 3:4–9). Some were healed by touching the person with the gift of healing (Luke 8:43–48; Acts 19:11–13). Others were also healed by prayer and anointing with oil (James 5:14–16).

The gift of faith is a supernatural faith the Holy Spirits gives to some believers to fulfill God's agenda. This type of faith is different from saving faith (Eph. 2:8–9; John 1:12–13; 3:14–15) and the faith we all need as believers to please God (Heb. 11:6). Saving faith and living faith can be nurtured to grow by constantly feeding and acting on God's Word (Rom. 10:17). On the other hand, the gift of faith is an extraordinary faith that "moves the mountains" of human problems in order to usher in God's eternal purposes.

Hardly does the gift of faith work in isolation; it usually operates hand in glove with other power gifts such as working of miracles and gifts of healings. In ministering healing to people, the Lord Jesus expected basic faith from the people who needed the ministry, but He had to exercise extraordinary faith to make the miracle happen—whether it was healing a withered hand, opening blind eyes, or raising Lazarus (who had been dead and buried three days prior) back to life. Peter and John exercised the gift of faith when they told the crippled man, "Look at us" and went ahead to command him to get up and walk (Acts 3:6–10).

Stephen performed miracles and wonders because he was "full of faith and power" (Acts 6:8). Healing and working of miracles sometimes come by perception of faith in the person in need of the blessing:

> In Lystra there sat a man who was lame. He had been that way from birth and had never walked. He listened to Paul as he was speaking. Paul looked directly at him, saw that he had faith to be healed and called out, "Stand up on your feet!" At that, the man jumped up and began to walk. (Acts 14:8 NIV, emphasis mine)

Because the gifts of power (and that matter all spiritual gifts) are for the total good of the church, they are made manifest in the congregation of God's people or where God's servants are. In the church, you may literally feel the power of God in your hands or body. People who touch you can attest to power being transferred to them. In some instances, people you are ministering to encounter the power of God flowing through you and fall under the power. They get up totally healed.

## Vocal Gifts

The vocal gifts comprise prophecy, diverse kinds of tongues, and interpretation of tongues. Prophecy refers to a supernatural utterance that is spoken to edify, exhort, and comfort believers (1 Cor. 14:13). Prophecy may also be described as receiving and disseminating divine revelation (Acts 13:1–5; 1 Cor. 14:26; 15:51; Rev. 2–3; 22:6–19). It is usually received during a time of personal or corporate worship, prayer, or in the course of preaching or teaching.

Once received, prophecy may be spoken extemporaneously or recorded in written form or recorded on audio for later dissemination. The gifts of prophecy described in 1 Corinthians chapter 12 and 14 appear to be received and spoken extemporaneously in the assembly of God's people. Old Testament prophecies—as well as prophetic aspects of Paul, Peter, and John—were all received and recorded in writing (Rev. 1:3; 1:9–11; 22:7, 9–10).

In addition to edification, exhortation, and comfort, prophecy may also foretell future events. In Acts 11:27–30, we read of a prophet called Agabus who predicted, by the Holy Spirit, that the entire world was going to experience a great famine.

> And in these days prophets came from Jerusalem to Antioch. Then one of them, named Agabus, stood up and showed by the Spirit that there was going to be a great famine throughout all the world, *which also happened in the days of Claudius Caesar.* Then the disciples, each according to his ability, determined to send relief to the brethren dwelling in Judea. This they also did, and sent it to

> the elders by the hands of Barnabas and Saul. (Acts 11:27–30 NKJV, emphasis mine)

It is important to note that the Bible says Agabus's prophecy was fulfilled during Emperor Claudius Caesar's reign. A test of Holy Spirit-inspired prophecy is that it must happen (Deut. 18:21–22; Jer. 28:9).

Another example of a New Testament prophecy that foretells the future is found in Acts 21:10–11.

> A certain prophet named Agabus came down from Judea. When he had come to us, he took Paul's belt, bound his own hands and feet, and said, "Thus says the Holy Spirit, 'So shall the Jews at Jerusalem bind the man who owns this belt, and deliver him into the hands of the Gentiles.'" (Acts 21:10–11 NKJV)

Moreover, the entire book of Revelation falls under the biblical classification of prophecy and foretells future events. Examples of people who prophesied in the New Testament prophets are Agabus (Acts 11:28; 21:10–11), the daughters of Philip (Acts 21:9), Judas, and Silas (Acts 15:32). Apart from the daughters of Philip, all the above-named disciples were prophets. All prophets prophesy, but not everyone who has the gift of prophecy is a prophet. Prophecy is a gift, but *prophet* is an office.

The gift of diverse kinds of tongues is the supernatural ability to speak, pray, or sing in a language unknown to or not learned by the speaker. There is a difference between the gift of diverse kinds of tongues as a gift of the Holy Spirit and speaking in tongues as the initial, visible manifestation of the baptism in the Holy Spirit. Both are supernatural, both are given by the Holy Spirit, and both involved speaking in an unknown language. However, while the latter is an initial sign of being filled with the Spirit and is available to every believer, the former is a gift the Holy Spirit gives to whoever He wills. The gift of diverse kinds of tongues may be exercised either in one's own private time of prayer or during corporate prayer.

How can you know you have the gift of diverse kinds of tongues? First, you will find yourself speaking in a tongue that is different from the tongues you normally hear yourself speaking in prayer. Two, you will find the pitch of your voice a little higher than normal and above others, and it will be a little hard to stop or control. Thus, when others stop praying, you have the opportunity to speak your message in tongues. If you have the gift of diverse kinds of tongues, the Bible encourages you to ask God for its companion gift: the gift of interpretation of tongues.

> So anyone who speaks in tongues should pray also for the ability to interpret what has been said. (1 Cor. 14:13 NLT)

The gift of interpretation of tongues is the supernatural ability to verbalize the meaning of a message spoken in an unknown language. It is supernatural because the person exercising the gift does not understand the language spoken in tongues but receives the meaning of the message spontaneously from the Holy Spirit. This is why it is supernatural. From my personal experience, the interpretation may come to you as a word theme, a phrase, or a sentence. As you speak forth the few pieces you received, the Holy Spirit unfolds more pieces to you. It is a step of faith. In other cases, the full interpretation comes to you while the other person is still speaking in tongues.

Sometimes people ask me, "How can I know I have the gift of interpretation of tongues?" Well, you may find yourself speaking the interpretation of your tongues during your private prayer or in corporate prayer sessions. As you pray, your normal prayer language will change to a different kind of tongue. Then, you will find yourself saying something in a language you understand as the Holy Spirit gives you utterance. That "something" you said, which you had no prior knowledge about, is the interpretation to the tongue you just spoke.

Now, a message spoken in tongues and interpreted in a known language is equivalent to prophecy. In mathematical terms:

Tongues + Interpretation of Tongues = Prophecy

## The Indispensable Role of the Holy Spirit in Regeneration

The word *regenerate* means to recreate, to be made anew, or to be born again. In John 3:3, Jesus stated that the prerequisite for entering God's kingdom is to be born again:

> Very truly I tell you, no one can see the kingdom of God unless they are born again. (John 3:3 NIV)

He also pointed out that regeneration is made possible when the Holy Spirit gives life to our human spirits.

> Jesus answered, "Very truly I tell you, no one can enter the kingdom of God unless they *are born of water and the Spirit.* Flesh gives birth to flesh, but the *Spirit gives birth to spirit.* You should not be surprised at my saying, 'You must be born again.' The wind blows wherever it pleases. You hear its sound, but you cannot tell where it comes from or where it is going. So it is with everyone born of the Spirit." (John 3:5–8 NIV, emphasis mine)

Regeneration is made possible by the power of God's Word (as symbolized by water, Eph. 5:25) and the transforming power of the Holy Spirit. Thus, the Holy Spirit plays an indispensable role in our regeneration. Indeed, without the Holy Spirit, no one can be regenerated. I will illustrate with a hypothetical case.

Let us imagine a scenario in a large hospital where Mary, a

registered nurse, is working on the cardiac unit during the 3:00–11:00 p.m. shift. One of Mary's patients, John, suddenly suffers a cardiopulmonary arrest, and Mary quickly calls "Code Blue" on her pager. Within seconds, the "Code Team" (comprising specially trained doctors, nurses, and respiratory technologists) rushes to the scene and immediately begins the resuscitation process. Realizing that the patient is unresponsive to CPR, the "Code Team" shocks the patient's heart with an automated external defibrillator (AED). Unfortunately, the AED reads zero heart rate and zero pulse rate, signifying that John is unresponsive to external stimuli. His skin begins to turn blue. After further examination, the medical doctor declares John dead. A separation of spirit and body has occurred; John's spirit has gone to its maker, and his body will return to dust (Eccl. 12:7; James 2:26).

Like John (who came to the hospital with a chronic heart disease), every one of us came into this world with an "incurable disease" called *sinful nature*. Our perverted nature has erected a wall of separation between God (the source of life) and us. All human efforts at resuscitation have failed. The prognosis does not look good; we are spiritually dead and unresponsive to God (Eph. 2:1–2; Romans 6:23). But God, with whom nothing is impossible, intervenes with His all-powerful Word and Spirit and "shocks" our spiritually dead spirits back to life! This, in a nutshell, is the Gospel! (good news). This is how the Holy Spirit regenerates our dead spirits. This is what happens when we (our spirits) are born again.

## The Holy Spirit Convicts

After making our dead spirits sensitive and responsive to God, the Holy Spirit convicts us of sin and our need for the Savior in accordance with the Lord's promise:

> When He (the Holy Spirit) comes, *He will convict the world of its sin*, and of *God's righteousness*, and of the coming *judgment*. (John 16:8 NLT, emphasis mine)

The unregenerate person is a rebel; his heart is deceitful and desperately wicked (Jer. 17:9). As a result, the unregenerate person does not submit to God. However, when the unregenerate person comes under the conviction of the Holy Spirit, they become conscious of their inadequacies and need for God's mercy and grace.

The Holy Spirit confronts the unregenerate person with their own sin and guilt and helps them acknowledge their sin, shortcomings, and need for the Savior. This truth is amply exemplified on the day of Pentecost. After Peter had delivered his Spirit-inspired message, his audience "were pricked in their heart, and said unto Peter and to the rest of the apostles, Men and brethren, what shall we do?" (Acts 2:37 KJV). The phrase "they were pricked in their heart" means they were deeply convicted of their sin and guilt as well as their need for the Savior. It was the Holy Spirit who used Peter's words to bring these unregenerate people under such deep conviction.

The Holy Spirit also convicts the unregenerate person of Christ's righteousness. He reveals to the sinner that, on the cross, Jesus exchanged His righteousness for our sinfulness so that we can become the righteousness of God (2 Cor. 5:21). By raising Jesus from the dead and sending the Holy Spirit to earth, God demonstrated His approval of Jesus as God's anointed Savior and Lord (Acts 2:33). The Holy Spirit exalts Christ in the eyes of the convicted sinner and helps the sinner to accept the Lordship of Christ.

Additionally, the Holy Spirit convicts the unregenerate person of judgment. The Holy Spirit opens the eyes of the understanding of the convicted person that Satan (the prince of this world) has been judged (defeated) and Jesus has been exalted "far above all principality, and power, and might, and dominion, and every name that is named, not only in this world, but also in that which is to come" (Eph. 1:21 KJV).

## The Holy Spirit Gives Life

Romans 8:11 tells us that the same Spirit who raised Jesus from the dead gives life to our mortal bodies. In, Jesus identifies the Holy Spirit and the Word of God as sources of life:

> *The Spirit* alone *gives eternal life.* Human effort accomplishes nothing. And the very *words* I have spoken to you *are* spirit and *life.* (John 6:63 NLT, emphasis mine)

The Holy Spirit give us life, renews our human spirit, and makes it responsive to Him:

> He (God) saved us, not because of righteous things we had done, but because of His mercy. He saved us through the washing of rebirth and renewal by the Holy Spirit. (Titus 3:5 NIV)

## The Holy Spirit Lives in Us

As discussed in chapter 3, only priests, kings, prophets, and few other leaders were anointed with the Holy Spirit before Pentecost. However, in the church age, the Lord is graciously pouring out His Spirit upon all people, irrespective of age, gender, geographical background, socioeconomic status, or educational level (Acts 2:16–18; Joel 2:28–29). Just as the Lord Jesus promised, the Holy Spirit now indwells every born-again believer:

> Don't you realize that your body is the temple of the Holy Spirit, who lives in you and was given to you by God? You do not belong to yourself. (1 Cor. 6:19 NLT)

In the Greek text, "you" and "your" are singular, indicating that the Holy Spirit has taken residence in each believer. The word "temple" here means tabernacle, house, residence, or dwelling place. So, if you are a born-again believer, your body is the residence of the Holy Spirit. Since the Holy Spirit is holy, He cannot live in an unholy person. Therefore, He makes you holy by cleansing you and setting you apart for His exclusive use.

It is worthy of note that the Holy Spirit also lives in the Church as a corporate body. Metaphorically, the Church is the Body of Christ with Jesus as the head and Lord. Jesus exercises His Lordship over the Church through the Holy Spirit.

> For *the Lord is the Spirit,* and *wherever the Spirit of the Lord is,* there is freedom. (2 Cor. 3:17 NLT, emphasis mine)

In other words, wherever the Spirit is allowed to be Lord, there is freedom.

**Your Personal Teacher**

The Holy Spirit lives in you for several strategic reasons. First, the Holy Spirit resides in you to be your personal teacher:

> You have received the Holy Spirit, and he lives within you, so you don't need anyone to teach you what is true. For the Spirit teaches you everything you need to know, and what He teaches is true—it is not a lie. So, just as He has taught you, remain in fellowship with Christ. (1 John 2:27 NLT, emphasis mine)

It is clear from the scripture above that the Holy Spirit is your personal teacher. He lives in you to teach you and to protect you from error. You can trust what the Holy Spirit teaches you because He is God and so He cannot lie (Num. 23:19; Heb. 6:18).

The Holy Spirit living inside you is eager to teach you, but you must be thirsty to drink from the streams of the living water. Before you open the pages the scriptures, you must sincerely ask the Holy Spirit to interpret God's Word to you. Since the Holy Spirit is the author of the scriptures, there is no better interpreter of God's Word than Him (2 Tim 3:15; 2 Pet. 1:21).

The Holy Spirit alone knows the original meaning of the words He inspired the writers of the scriptures to write. So, yield control of your mind and spirit to Him and let Him break the fresh bread of life to you.

## Your Personal Guide

Another reason why the Holy Spirit resides in you is to guide you:

> When the Spirit of truth comes, He will guide you into all truth. He will not speak on his own but will tell you what He has heard. He will tell you about the future. (John 16:13 NLT)

I never cease to be amazed by the similarities between how the GPS functions and how the Holy Spirit guides us. The GPS leads and directs us to unknown places by detecting satellite signals in the atmosphere. It can detect traffic, accidents, police presence, and road construction a mile away and suggest alternate routes. We have the option to select the GPS-recommended route or fall into the unpleasant situation the GPS warned us about. When we miss our exit, the GPS quickly recalibrates and brings us back to the right way. Sometimes, the GPS takes us through unfamiliar routes but ultimately gets us to our destination. My experience is that the GPS is about 97 percent reliable, and we will save ourselves lots of unnecessary headaches and delays if we follow the lead of the GPS.

Thankfully, living inside us as believers in Christ is the omniscient, all-loving, and infallible Holy Spirit, who is our personal guide and helper. Just as we rely on the GPS to guide us when driving, we must trust the Holy Spirit to guide us in life's journey. Unlike the GPS, however, which must be programmed and sometimes makes mistakes, the Holy Spirit is 100 percent capable, knows everything, and cannot make mistakes. He knows the end of a thing from the beginning, and His judgments are always right. As God's personal representative on earth, His work is to guide us through the exigencies of life.

The Holy Spirit is our most reliable Guide, Teacher, and ever-present Helper. He sees what we can't see with our natural senses and knows the best routes we must take in our life journeys. Sometimes, He nudges us to avoid our familiar shortcuts and points us to unfamiliar or longer routes. All we need to do is trust in His unmistakable judgment. He would not compel us to take His recommended route, but we are certainly better off when we choose to follow His leading.

Note: Please understand that I am not in any way trivializing the work of the Holy Spirit or saying that the Holy Spirit can be programmed like a GPS. Not at all.

**Your Personal Helper**

There are many more things the Holy Spirit does in our lives to ensure that we fulfill God's purpose for our lives. I will just describe this role of the Holy Spirit as help. The Holy Spirit's helping role includes strengthening us with inner power to live victoriously (Eph. 3:16), as God's seal or God's mark of authenticity and approval on us, and as a deposit guaranteeing our redemption as God's possession (Eph. 1:13–14). When we allow Him, the Holy Spirit continuously and consistently fills us (Eph. 5:18), anoints us (1 John 2:27), and sanctifies us (1 Pet. 1:2). The Holy Spirit gives us power and boldness to be Christ's witnesses (Acts 1:8; 1 Cor. 12:7–11; Rom. 12:4–8; 2 Tim. 1:7–8), helps us produce Christlike character (Gal. 5:22–23), gives life to our mortal bodies (Rom. 8:11), and makes the Gospel efficacious (1 Thess. 1:5).

## Prophetic Word Concerning the End-Time Church

In many parts of the world, churches have become mere monuments—a far cry from the first-century Church. God is not interested in monuments! He wants a movement! God is interested in people who are sold out for His kingdom interests. This is why He is raising up an army of mostly young people who are thirsty for what the first-century Church had. All over the world, the Holy Spirit is creating a new craving for the rivers of the Holy Spirit in the hearts of young people. These young people are being prepared to assume new leadership roles in what God is doing.

Mantels are falling! Mantels are falling before the present order phases out. God is raising layers of leadership. Three generations of spiritual mentors and mentees will exist concurrently. There is a shift in the spirit, and only those who align with the purposes of God can participate in what God is doing in the closing hours of the last days.

The end-time Church cannot finish by the flesh what the early Church began by the Spirit. Since the church was born by the power of the Holy Spirit, it must end by the same. The Church was inaugurated in power; in power, must it continue till it is raptured into glory!

# PART III
## How You Can Experience the Holy Spirit as Your Indispensable Friend

# Chapter 10

## You Can Enjoy His Indispensable Fullness

*God wants us to step beyond the shores of salvation into the deep breakers of the supernatural.*

ONE OF THE THINGS I am really bad at doing is swimming. As a boy, while my friends were busy showing off their swimming skills, I was content to swim at the shore. As you can imagine, I was the object of constant jeering from my friends whenever we went to the beach. Tired of their teasing, one sunny day, I decided to put away my aquaphobia (fear of water) and followed my friends into the deep. To my surprise, I found myself actually swimming. As I looked at the vast expanse of the blue, calm Atlantic Ocean, I couldn't help but say to myself, "Wow! Swimming is not as scary as I thought."

Analogically, the Holy Spirit can be likened to the ocean—huge and mostly unexplored. Like the ocean, there are innumerable treasures in the Holy Spirit. There are limitless untapped resources in the Holy Spirit. Unfortunately, like me, most Christians are just content to be "swimming at the shore." Most Christians have not experienced even the "glimpses of glory" a fraction of believers experience from time to time. Most Christians seem satisfied with the occasional "stirrings of the waters" of the Holy Spirit instead of tapping into the fullness of the Holy Spirit. In this closing chapter, I will address three critical questions. First, what does it mean to be full of the Holy Spirit? Second, why is important to experience the fullness of the Holy Spirit? Third, why are so many Christians not experiencing the fullness of the Holy Spirit?

## Fullness of the Holy Spirit

There is so much more in the Holy Spirit for us to experience. At the risk of sounding tautologous, there is so much more in the Holy Spirit we have not experienced yet. There is so much more in the Holy Spirit we don't even know exists. The Holy Spirit is much more than we can ever imagine. He is infinite in love, grace, peace, joy, and wisdom. In the Spirit of the LORD, we have a treasure trove of supernatural wisdom, understanding, counsel, strength, knowledge, and fear of the LORD (Isa. 11:2). His resources—such as gifts, character, fruit, power, and ministries—are readily available to anyone who would tap into them.

God wants us to step beyond the shores of salvation into the deep breakers of the supernatural. God wants us to experience the "deep things of God" that can only be revealed to us by the Holy Spirit (1 Cor. 2:10). All that the Holy Spirit has is meant to be released through us for the exaltation of Jesus and to the glory of the Father.

> **Remember**
>
> *God wants us to step beyond the shores of salvation into the deep breakers of the supernatural.*

Since I have been espousing the idea that God wants us to experience the fullness of the Holy Spirit, it is incumbent on me to explain what I mean by the phrase "fullness of the Holy Spirit." By way of illustration, imagine a cup that is full of water. That cup is completely filled (occupied) with water. The cup has no more room for any other substance to fill. Similarly, when you are full of the Holy Spirit, you are totally filled with the Holy Spirit. The spirit-filled person is completely controlled or led by the Holy Spirit. In other words, you are full of the Holy Spirit if you are consistently controlled by the Holy Spirit. God wants His children to be filled with the Holy Spirit at all times. Being filled with the Holy Spirit should not be sporadic; it should be a lifestyle.

> **Remember**
>
> *All that the Holy Spirit has is meant to be released through us for the exaltation of Jesus and to the glory of the Father.*

## Why Does God Want Us to Be Filled with the Holy Spirit?

### I: Consistent Portrayal of God

God wants His children to be constantly filled with the Holy Spirit to ensure a consistent, spirit-filled lifestyle. An inconsistent lifestyle can send mixed messages about our Lord to the unbelieving world. It gives a distorted view of God to the world. People get confused about the true nature of our faith and our God when we demonstrate godly character some of the time and live like anybody else at other times. A fountain does not send out both sweet and bitter water, and neither does a fig produce vine berries (James 3:11–12). Just as light and darkness have nothing in common, Christians are supposed to distinguish themselves from others by their godly character; this can only happen if we are consistently filled with the Holy Spirit.

### II: It Makes Us Ever Productive

The spirit-filled Christian automatically manifests the unique characteristics of the Holy Spirit such as wisdom, understanding, knowledge, and fear of the Lord (Isaiah 11:2). If you are full of the Holy Spirit, you will demonstrate the fruit of the Spirit such as love, joy, peace, goodness, faithfulness, gentleness, and self-control in your life (Gal. 5:22–23). Spirit-filled people do not need to make extra effort to produce fruit consistent with God's character because "against such there is no law" (Gal. 5:23 NIV). They have "crucified the flesh with its passions and desires" and "live by the Spirit" (Gal. 5:24–25).

### III: It Makes Our Testimony Effective

A consistent spirit-filled lifestyle makes our Christian testimony effective. How? When our lifestyles consistently align with our professions, it makes our Christian testimonies strong and effective. Like Daniel, the only grounds of accusation will be with respect to our faith and not for wrongdoing.

> The administrators and the satraps tried to find grounds for charges against Daniel in his conduct of government affairs, but they were unable to do so. They could find no corruption in him, because he was trustworthy and neither corrupt nor negligent. Finally these men said, "We will never find any basis for charges against this man Daniel unless it has something to do with the law of his God." (Dan. 6:4–5 NIV)

### IV: Additional Blessings

A person who is full of the Holy Spirit will be a bold witness for Christ, will exercise the gifts of

---

*Remember*

*A person who is full of the Holy Spirit will be a bold witness for Christ, will exercise the gifts of the Spirit, and will demonstrate the God kind of love to all manner of people.*

the Spirit, and will demonstrate the God kind of love to all manner of people (Acts 1:8; 1 Corinthians 12:7–11; Romans 5:5). Let us analyze the lives of our Lord Jesus and Stephen, the first Christian martyr, as cases studies of people who were filled with the Holy Spirit.

## Example of Jesus

> Jesus, *full of the Holy Spirit*, left the Jordan and was *led by the Spirit* into the wilderness; where for forty days he was tempted by the devil. (Luke 4:1 NIV, emphasis mine)

This passage of scripture affirms the truth we established earlier that being full of the Holy Spirit is synonymous with being led by the Spirit. When you are led by the Spirit, you are controlled by the Spirit—not by force but by voluntary submission.

It is also significant to note that it was the Holy Spirit who led Jesus into the wilderness to be tempted by the devil (Matt. 4:1 NIV). This shows that being full of the Holy Spirit can take us to challenging situations. The Holy Spirit can lead you away from your comfort zone into tough situations—not to crush you but to prepare you for greater works.

If the Holy Spirit led the beloved Son of God into the wilderness to be tempted by the devil, you can be sure we will also have our "wilderness experience" in one way or another. Jesus was able to overcome the devil's temptations in the wilderness because He was full of the Holy Spirit, he was saturated with the scriptures, and he maintained unbroken fellowship with the Father. If we want to experience a victorious lifestyle, we must learn from our Master.

## Example of Stephen

When the leaders of the first-century Church needed men to oversee administrative duties, they looked for men with proven character, full of the Holy Spirit, and full of wisdom (Acts 6:3). They wanted men who had demonstrated a lifestyle of integrity, total obedience to the Holy Spirit, and the ability to make wise decisions.

Stephen, one of the seven men chosen for this responsibility, was described as "a man *full of faith and of the Holy Spirit*" (Acts 6:5 NIV, emphasis mine). He was also labeled as "a man *full of God's grace and power*, who performed great wonders and signs among the people" (Acts 6:8 NIV, emphasis mine). Again, in Acts 7:55, Stephen was described as a man "full of the Holy Spirit."

Stephen demonstrated Christlike characteristics all the way to his death:

> While they were stoning him, Stephen prayed, "Lord Jesus, receive my spirit." Then he fell on his knees and cried out, "Lord, do not hold this sin against them." When he had said this, he fell asleep. (Acts 7:59–60 NIV)

By praying for the forgiveness of his murderers, Stephen demonstrated the God kind of love, grace, and mercy, reminiscent of the Lord Jesus, who on the cross of Crucifixion cried out, "Father, forgive them, for they do not know what they are doing" (Luke 23:34). The gracious spirit Stephen demonstrated attests to the fact that he was indeed full of the Holy Spirit.

## Why Don't We Experience the Fullness of the Holy Spirit?

There may be many reasons why most Christians don't experience the fullness of the Holy Spirit, but I believe there are three main reasons for this situation: ignorance, misinformation, and lack of understanding. All three factors are interrelated. Ignorance of the truth can make you vulnerable to misinformation, which can lead to lack of understanding of the truth.

## I: Ignorance

I believe a sizeable percent of Christians do not know that God wants us to experience personal, intimate relationships with the Holy Spirit. I dare say that most Christians do not have experiential knowledge of the Holy Spirit's leading, teaching, and revelation of God's will with respect to a particular situation. Most Christians I know are shocked when I tell them that they can (individually) develop a personal relationship with the Holy Spirit.

This ignorance about our relationship with the Holy Spirit is a reflection of a bigger problem of lack of experiential knowledge of God, which comes from spending quality time in God's presence. Sadly, increasing numbers of Christians have forsaken the foundational habits of personal Bible study and prayer.[2] In America, the percentage of church-attending, self-professing Christians who read their Bibles consistently continues to dwindle (Stetzer, 2014) as shown in the following data:

| Frequency of Bible Reading | Percent |
| --- | --- |
| Daily | 19% |
| A few times a week | 26% |
| Once a week | 14% |
| At least once a month | 22% |
| Rarely or never | 18% |

Meanwhile, 90 percent of homes in America have a Bible; the average American home has three Bibles, not counting electronic Bibles and downloadable Bible apps on mobile devices. Isn't it ironic that the more Bibles we acquire (both printed and electronic), the less we read them and the more ignorant we become of the author

---

[2] https://www.christianitytoday.com/edstetzer/2014/october/biblical-illiteracy-by-numbers.html

of the Bible? Lack of basic Bible knowledge erodes the essential soil on which the Holy Spirit can sow the seeds of revelation.

The Lord laments, "My people are being destroyed because they don't know me (Hos. 4:6 NLT, emphasis mine)." In Hosea's time, lack of knowledge of the Holy Spirit stemmed from rejection of God's truth by the religious leaderships. Could it be the same today?

## II: Misinformation

Many Christians don't experience the fullness of the Holy Spirit due to misinformation. In some circles of contemporary Christianity, there is the general notion that only certain "men of God" are "anointed" enough to hear from God or are capable of walking in the fullness of the Holy Spirit. This is an Old Testament concept. In the Old Testament, only kings, prophets, and priests (and sometimes people divinely ordained for special duties such as Bezalel) were filled with the Holy Spirit to perform their God-ordained functions. The rest of the people, therefore, had to seek God's direction through these anointed men.

Truth is, God has indeed anointed certain people for their special assignments in His kingdom (Eph. 4:11–14). Additionally, New Testament believers have unhindered access to God through the Holy Spirit who dwells in us. God's promise to pour His Spirit on all flesh was given in the Old Testament.

Through Old Testament prophets like Isaiah, Habakkuk, and Jeremiah, the LORD promised to establish a new covenant with His people under which each believer would be able to follow God's commands through their personal relationship with the Holy Spirit. For example, in Jeremiah chapter 33, the LORD gave the following profound promise to Israel:

> "This is the *new covenant* I will make with the people of Israel on that day," says the LORD. "I will put my instructions deep within them, and I will write them on their hearts. *I will be their God, and they will be*

*my people.* And they will not need to teach their neighbors, nor will they need to teach their relatives, saying, 'You should know the LORD.' *For everyone, from the least to the greatest, will know me* already," says the LORD. "And I will forgive their wickedness, and I will never again remember their sins." It is the LORD who provides the sun to light the day and the moon and stars to light the night, and who stirs the sea into roaring waves. His name is the LORD of Heaven's Armies, and this is what he says: "I am as likely to reject my people Israel as I am to abolish the laws of nature!" (Jer. 31:33–36 NLT, emphasis mine)

In this prophecy, the LORD promises to gather the scattered people of Israel back to their land as one nation. God reminds them that just as He commands the sun to light the day and the moon and stars to light the night—and they obey—His promise will be fulfilled. He points to His faithfulness in maintaining the laws of nature to assure Israel that He will keep His promise. Now, in this prophecy to bring Israel back to its land, God promises to establish a new covenant (New Testament) with His people. The New Testament would be based on the foundation of:

- A relationship (not rules): "I will be *their God* and they will be *my people*" (Jer. 31:33 NLT, emphasis mine).
- New birth: "I will give you a *new heart* and put a *new spirit in you*; I will remove from you your heart of stone and give you a heart of flesh" (Ezek. 36:26 NIV, emphasis mine). "I will put my instructions deep within them, and I will write them on their hearts (Jer. 31:33 NLT).
- Forgiveness of sin: "I will forgive their wickedness, and I will never again remember their sins" (Jer. 31:34 NIV).
- Spirit-empowered grace: "I will put my Spirit in you and move you to follow my decrees and be careful to keep my laws" (Ezek. 36:27 NIV).

The Lord predicts that this New Covenant blessing is for all people: "Afterward, I will pour out my Spirit on all people (Joel 2:28 NIV, emphasis mine).

The writer of the Epistle to the Hebrews applied the promise of the New Covenant to all people who have covenant relationship with God through faith in the finished work of Jesus Christ:

> The New Testament (Covenant) is established on better promises. For, if there had been nothing wrong with that first covenant, no place would have been sought for another. But God found fault with the people and said: "The days are coming, declares the Lord, when I will make a new covenant with the people of Israel and with the people of Judah. It will not be like the covenant I made with their ancestors when I took them by the hand to lead them out of Egypt, because they did not remain faithful to my covenant, and I turned away from them," declares the Lord. "This is the covenant I will establish with the people of Israel after that time," declares the Lord. "I will put my laws in their minds and write them on their hearts. I will be their God, and they will be my people. No longer will they teach their neighbor, or say to one another, 'Know the Lord,' because they will all know me, from the least of them to the greatest. For I will forgive their wickedness and will remember their sins no more." By calling this covenant "new," he has made the first one obsolete; and what is obsolete and outdated will soon disappear. (Heb. 8:6–13 NIV)

In the New Covenant, God wants "the earth to be filled with the knowledge of the glory of the Lord as the waters cover the sea (Hab. 2:14; Isa. 11:9). God has given New Testament believers His Spirit (anointing) to know the truth (1 John 2:20).

> But you have received the Holy Spirit, and he lives within you, so you don't need anyone to teach you what is true. For the Spirit teaches you everything you need to know, and what he teaches is true—it is not a lie. So, just as He has taught you, remain in fellowship with Christ. (1 John 2:27 NLT)

Other versions of the Bible use "the anointing" in place of "the Holy Spirit." The bottom line is that while God has indeed given certain people special anointing for their special callings, all born-again believers in Christ have received the Holy Spirit ("the anointing") to instruct us and order our steps through life's journey. Our responsibility is to cultivate our relationship with the Holy Spirit so we can experience His fullness as individuals.

## III: Lack of Understanding

There is a huge difference between knowledge and understanding. Knowledge is gained through acquaintance with facts, principles, truth, or familiarity with a subject or learning. On the other hand, we gain understanding when we exercise our mental faculties to comprehend, interpret, or discern something or a situation. For example, though Jesus repeatedly told His disciples that He would be crucified and rise from the dead on the third day, His disciples did not understand it. Even after His resurrection, Jesus's disciples had difficulty believing that He had indeed resurrected from the dead. Finally, He appeared to a large group of His disciples, bid them God's peace, and showed His pierced hands, feet, and sides. To demonstrate that He was a real human being, He ate in front of them. He also explained to them that His Crucifixion and resurrection were in fulfillment of what the prophets had foretold. The Lord then did something very significant:

> Then He opened their minds so they could understand the scriptures. He told them, This is

> what is written: The Messiah will suffer and rise from the dead on the third day, and repentance for the forgiveness of sins will be preached in his name to all nations, beginning at Jerusalem. You are witnesses of these things. I am going to send you what my Father has promised; but stay in the city until you have been clothed with power from on high." (Luke 24:45–49 NIV)

Though the disciples had knowledge of the scriptures, they lacked understanding. Until the Lord opened their understanding, they could not comprehend, interpret, or relate the Crucifixion and resurrection to the overall purpose of God for our redemption and the salvation of the humanity.

The Lord quickly linked His redemptive work to the necessity for the preaching of repentance for the forgiveness of sins and the role of the Holy Spirit to accomplish this mission. As soon as the Holy Spirit fell on the disciples on the day of Pentecost, however, Peter and the other disciples immediately understood the scriptures concerning Jesus's death, resurrection, repentance, and receiving of the Holy Spirit:

> "God has made this Jesus whom you crucified, both Lord and Messiah." When the people heard this, they were cut to the heart and said to Peter and the other apostles, "Brothers, what shall we do?" Peter replied, "Repent and be baptized, every one of you, in the name of Jesus Christ for the forgiveness of your sins. And you will receive the gift of the Holy Spirit. The promise is for you and your children and for all who are far off—for all whom the Lord our God will call." ... Those who accepted his message were baptized, and about three thousand were added to their number that day. (Acts 2:36–39, 41 NIV)

*The Holy Spirit*

The same disciples who had trouble understanding and believing the scriptures could now make complete sense of the scriptures when they were filled with the Holy Spirit. What the intellectuals could not comprehend was revealed to "babes" and uneducated (Luke 10:21). The Jewish leaders disdained the disciples for their lack of formal education and low socioeconomic status, but they could not deny the power the disciples demonstrated:

> Now *when they saw the boldness of Peter and John,* and *perceived that they were unlearned* and ignorant men, they marvelled; and they took knowledge of them, that they had been with Jesus. And beholding the man which was healed standing with them, they could say nothing against it. But when they had commanded them to go aside out of the council, they conferred among themselves, Saying, What shall we do to these men? For that indeed *a notable miracle hath been done by them is manifest* to all them that dwell in Jerusalem; and *we cannot deny it.* (Acts 4:13–16 KJV, emphasis mine)

The third reason why people are unable to tap into the fullness of the Holy Spirit is because they want to understand spiritual things with their natural minds. That is impossible because spiritual things are spiritually discerned (1 Cor. 2:14). The religious leaders were the best intellectual minds of the day, yet they realized that Jesus's disciples, who had little or no formal education, would not be intimated by their intellectual and religious pedigree. Unable to reconcile the apostles' "ignorance," boldness, and ability to perform miraculous acts, the Jewish leaders marveled at the wisdom and understanding of the apostles. They then understood that these disciples had been with Jesus (Acts 4:13).

It is the same today. Many highly educated people, including professors of theology, deny the operations of the Holy Spirit that are clearly revealed in scripture while less educated people, who receive scripture with the simplicity of a little child, are tapping into the awesome power and glory of the Holy Spirit. Ability to tap into the fullness of the Spirit does not depend on one's education or the lack thereof. It just depends on divine revelation and understanding that come by total submission to the Holy Spirit, our indispensable Teacher, Helper, and Guide.

The two pillars of the first-century church, Peter and Paul, were on opposite ends of the educational spectrum, yet both of them learned to tap into the fullness of the Holy Spirit. Peter did not allow his lack of education prevent him from depending on the Holy Spirit. Paul, despite his high educational attainment, refused to lean on his own brilliance. Instead, he chose to rely totally on the irresistible power of the Holy Spirit:

> And so it was with me, brothers and sisters. When I came to you, I did not come with eloquence or human wisdom as I proclaimed to you the testimony about God. For I resolved to know nothing while I was with you except Jesus Christ and him crucified. I came to you in weakness with great fear and trembling. My message and my preaching were not with wise and persuasive words, but with a demonstration of the Spirit's power, so that your faith might not rest on human wisdom, but on God's power. (1 Cor. 2:1–5 NIV, emphasis mine)

The lesson is simple. God is able to use anyone irrespective of their status in life. Our responsibility is to humbly but actively ask the Holy Spirit for power to live victoriously and for effective ministry. Education or the lack thereof is not a requirement for experiencing the fullness of the Holy Spirit. The requirement for experiencing the fullness of the Holy Spirit is to empty ourselves of every trace of self-dependence and actively and sincerely ask the Holy Spirit to fill us till we overflow. That is God's best for each one of His children.

# Chapter 11

## Be Led by the Indispensable Spirit

*Our ability to hear God's voice, discern the move of God, and be part of what God is doing depends on how intimate our relationship with the Holy Spirit is.*

It seemed like any other summer afternoon. A comfortable breeze pierced the hot air. Stella was grateful to have had her "big" grocery done and was glad to be heading back to her small restaurant. Monday was her off day, but she hardly got time to rest since it was also the day she restocked her pantry.

As Stella drove down the Providence-Worcester Turnpike from Rhode Island toward Massachusetts, "something inside" her was urging her to pray. Not knowing what to pray about, she just brushed the thought aside. To her surprise, the nudge wouldn't go away. The more she tried to brush it aside, the stronger the urge to pray became. Reluctantly and not sure what to pray about, she began to pray—in tongues. Once she started, she realized she couldn't stop praying as the Holy Spirit took over and led her to pray for about ten minutes. She then found herself praising the Lord in English.

Suddenly, she heard a loud noise on the rear right side. Initially, she thought it was a gunshot, but it turned out to be a burst tire. Her left front tire had burst! Having lost control of her fully loaded Ford Transit-250 van, all Stella could do was to scream, "Jesus! Jesus! Jesus!" Miraculously, the car meandered its way through the other cars and came to a stop on the shoulder of the road—as if guided by an invisible angelic hand.

All too often, I hear Christians say, "Something inside me told me to do so and so. I wish I had acted on that prompting." This statement reveals that many Christians don't know the "prompting inside them" might be the voice of the Holy Spirit. Learning to discern the voice of the Holy Spirit is one of the most important disciplines every Christian must develop. The invention of the GPS should inform us about what the eternal, omnipresent, and omniscient Holy Spirit is capable of doing in our lives, especially with respect to guidance.

Truth is, God does speak to us through His Spirit, and it is up to us, as His children, to learn to discern and respond to the voice of the Holy Spirit. God does not want us to be in the dark. As children of light, we are not supposed to walk in the dark (ignorance) but in the light (revelation of God's will). As we discussed earlier, one of the primary ministries of the Holy Spirit is to lead or guide believers in Christ (John 16:26). We grow spiritually into God's mature children when we consistently allow the Holy Spirit to lead us (Rom. 8:14).

If we want to be led by the Holy Spirit, we need to keep quite a few things in mind. For example, we must remind ourselves of His characteristics, especially His personality. The Holy Spirit is a person. He can be related with. He can speak to us. He can guide us. He is willing to teach us if we allow Him, and He can be grieved if we ignore His promptings. We must, therefore, expect to hear the voice of the Holy Spirit. More importantly, we must create opportunities to hear Him.

As individuals, we must learn to develop personal relationships with the Holy Spirit. Like all relationships, we must expect open dialogue with the Holy Spirit. As the lesser partner in the relationship, we must learn to defer to the promptings of the Holy Spirit in all matters pertaining to life, ministry, and eternity.

We must also remember that the Holy Spirit is God's personal representative on earth to help us in every aspect of our lives. We must, therefore, learn to relate to the Him with reverence as Lord. In this chapter, I will share some simple, practical steps to help position yourself for the Holy Spirit to lead you.

## Spend Quality Time with Him

Our walk with the Holy Spirit demands spending quality time with Him. As I stated in chapter 5, any relationship worth its sort must be nurtured through intimate, unbroken fellowship, open communication, and mutual commitment. I hear people say, "I'm so busy. I don't have time to spend with God." Well, if it's important, you will make time for it. Hearing God's voice should be the highest priority for every child of God. The Holy Spirit is always available and ready for one-on-one fellowship with us. We have to make time for Him.

When you open your life to the Holy Spirit, He will reveal the mysteries of God to you. God will delight in you and entrust you with the precious secrets of His kingdom. You will become privy to the mind of God. God will give you access to the corridors of spiritual power, authority, and influence.

There are two primary ways by which we can develop quality relationship with the Holy Spirit: through study of God's written Word and prayer. When we read the Bible, God speaks to us—and the Holy Spirit interprets the Word for us. Thus, the Holy Spirit makes the Word come alive and become applicable to our circumstances. Prayer is the means by which we are able to talk to God. In prayer, the Holy Spirit again is our intercessor-in-chief. He shows us what we must pray about and prays through us. I will throw more light on these powerful opportunities God has granted us to maximize our relationship with Him.

## Get to Know Him from the Scriptures

Whenever we open the Bible, we must remember that the Holy Spirit is the Author of the scriptures, and if we ask Him, He will explain and interpret the scriptures for us (2 Tim. 3:16). He is the expert, and we are the protégés. The Holy Spirit will use the scriptures to reveal the sins we must confess, the examples we must emulate, our blessings in Christ—and how to appropriate them—and our assignments on earth. If you are intentional about it, you will get to know the Holy Spirit as your personal guide and teacher (John 14:16, 26). From the pages of scripture, the Holy Spirit will reveal the secrets of God's heart and mind to you. You will experience Him every time you open the Bible to read.

Saturate your heart and mind with the infallible Word of God through daily study, memorizing, and meditation on the scriptures. Then, out of your scripture-saturated heart will proceed thoughts and words that are in harmony with God's Word (Matt. 12:34). Your faith will increase if you saturate your heart with God's Word (Rom. 10:17). The scriptures in you will be life to you and health to your whole body (Prov. 4:22 NIV). God's Word will cleanse your heart (John 15:3) and sanctify your soul (2 Thess. 2:13). Studying and obeying the Word of God renews your mind. Your renewed mind and sanctified spirit will position you to receive guidance from the Holy Spirit. It's just a matter of course.

## Maintain a Lifestyle of Prayer

Maintain a lifestyle of unbroken prayer and worship if you are determined to be led by the Holy Spirit. Edify yourself by praying with your spirit (in tongues) daily. Revere Him by being conscious of His presence with you all the time. Talk with Him about everything—your fears and concerns—and ask Him to talk to you. Ask Him to reveal the prophetic purposes of God to you. Pray in faith. The more answered prayers you get, the more confident you become that your prayers will be answered. Pray till you feel a release in your spirit and learn to hear His voice

Ask the Holy Spirit to lead you. Determine never to worry about anything—and pray about everything (Ph. 4:6). Indeed, the Bible encourages us to ask God for guidance (wisdom) if we need it (James 1:5–7). You must acknowledge your need for guidance (lack of wisdom), sincerely desire to be led by the Holy Spirit, and ask God the Holy Spirit to show you what you must do. You must also ask in faith and expect to receive the direction you requested from the Holy Spirit.

It is important to be prepared to follow the direction the Holy Spirit gives you—usually one step at a time. The Lord's guidance is usually stepwise (Ps. 119:105). God hardly reveals the entire picture to us. However, as you take the first step, He will unfold the subsequent steps to you. If you don't take the first step, He will not give you more light.

To be effective, our prayer must originate from God and be energized by the Holy Spirit. There are at least four kinds of Holy Spirit-energized prayers: namely prayers that are directly based on God's Word, prayers that are directly inspired by the Holy Spirit, prayers that are spontaneously spoken in an unknown language, and travailing prayer. In line with Eph. 5:19, we must learn to pray in the Spirit at all times with all kinds of prayers and supplications.

In our prayers, we must consistently defer to God's will. Like Mary, our hearts' cry should be: "I am the Lord's servant. May everything you have said about me come true" (Luke 1:38 NLT). Jesus is our supreme example of a life that is totally yielded to God's will. When faced with imminent suffering and death, our Lord prayed, "Father, if you are willing, take this cup from me; yet *not my will, but yours be done*" (Luke 22:42 NIV, emphasis mine).

Moreover, when the Holy Spirit prompts us to pray and we don't know what to pray about, we must open our mouths and trust God to fill it with the right prayer (Ps. 81:10). We can also shift to our supernatural prayer language and pray with our spirits as the Holy Spirit carries us along. The Holy Spirit can also inspire us to travail in prayer. Travailing prayer is necessary for "spiritual childbirth" just as, in the natural, travail is necessary for giving birth to a child. Travailing prayer may or may not involve words, but it always involves a deep burden for which we must intercede till it is birthed (realized).

Patiently waiting for the answer to our prayer is another essential discipline we need to develop if we want to be led by the Spirit. Wait patiently for the Lord. Be brave and courageous. Yes, wait patiently for the LORD (Ps. 27:14 NLT). Twice in this verse, the Bible commands us to wait patiently for the LORD. Learning to listen for the voice of the Holy Spirit is a process. It demands our full attention and time. Restaurant waitresses don't rush their guests; they wait on them. Waiting on the Lord to receive divine guidance must be done intentionally, with courtesy, and without rush.

If you wait patiently for the Lord, He will incline His ear to your cry and answer you (Ps. 40:1). No one who waits for the Lord is ever put to shame (Ps. 25:3). The Lord always shows up and gives me a sure word whenever I patiently wait on Him. When I stay my mind on Him and ask Him to give guidance, He always speaks to me from within me or through the scriptures. Often, it is not spectacular, but it is always authoritative.

**Get to Know Him Experientially**

It is not enough to know the Holy Spirit from the scriptures; you must get to know him experientially. Jesus said, "My sheep *hear my voice*, and I know them, and *they follow me*" (John 10:27 KJV, emphasis mine). "But *they will never follow a stranger*; in fact, *they will run away from him* because *they do not recognize a stranger's voice*" (John 10:5 NIV, emphasis mine).

Since Jesus has been replaced by the Holy Spirit on earth, He expects His sheep (Christians) to recognize (hear) the voice of the Holy Spirit and follow Him. Hearing the voice of the Holy Spirit and following His lead, therefore, is a distinctive mark of

*The Holy Spirit*

the mature child of God (Rom. 8:14). Another distinctive mark of a mature child of God is that he or she neither recognizes nor follows the voice of imposters (false spirits, false Christs, and false teachers). In fact, mature children of God flee from all other voices!

As a boy, I used to accompany my grandmother as she took her sheep to the fields for grazing. She would lead the sheep with a croaky sound, and the sheep (including the straying ones) would come running after her. Grandma's sheep even responded to their names when she called them. Like sheep, we are prone to going astray. Fortunately, God leads us by the gentle voice of His Spirit. Our responsibility, therefore, is to train our human spirits to hear the voice of the Holy Spirit and follow His voice. People sometimes ask me, "What is the voice of the Holy Spirit like?"

My personal experience with the Holy Spirit is that His voice is gentle but authoritative. He does not yell or shout. Instead, He speaks with such clarity and authority that I never have any doubt in my heart that it *is* His voice. In most cases, the voice of the Holy Spirit appears to come from within me. The voice of the Holy Spirit is usually spontaneous and illuminating. He never condemns. He only encourages—even when He is pointing out a sin in my life. It's almost like the Holy Spirit is more interested in lifting me out of the dark pit of rejection than pushing me into the dungeon of condemnation. His voice is always refreshing, endearing, and welcoming. That's how I know it's the voice of the Holy Spirit.

Again, from both personal experience and scripture, I have learned that the guidance of the Holy Spirit is not foggy. It is never ambiguous; it is always clear. God is light, and in Him, there is no darkness at all (1 John 1:5 NIV). When you ask God for guidance, you must ask Him to make it as clear and unambiguous as daylight. You must tell God you are willing to do His will if He will show it to you. He is a covenant-keeping God. He will keep His promise and guide you.

## Develop Sensitivity to Him

I have also learned that if we desire to be led by the Holy Spirit, we must be sensitive to Him, His voice, and His ways. This requires waiting in His presence. The Lord says, "Be still and know that I am God" (Ps. 46:10 NIV).

Developing sensitivity to the Holy Spirit may mean getting away from the hustles of life and setting time aside to hear what the Holy Spirit has to tell you. If may require shutting off your radio while driving and allowing your spirit to communion with Him. You must be ready to hear from Him. Waiting on the Holy Spirit goes hand-in-hand with maintaining an attitude of expectancy. You must be intentional about it. You must learn to "shut yourself away" from the world and "shut yourself in" in the presence of God if you want to hear His voice.

I learned this practice early in my Christian life as a teenager. My three older brothers and I shared one room when I was growing up. Most days when I woke up at dawn to pray, my brothers would be playing music: Bob Marley, the Commodores, or Jimmy Cliff. Since I had nowhere else to go and pray, I would just lie down on my flat student's mattress and pray quietly. In this unfavorable environment, I learned to "shut myself" away from the noise in the room and be "caught up" in the presence of Lord. The Holy Spirit would commune with me and reveal His plans for the day as I soaked myself in Him.

Whenever I traveled from one city to another, I would "shut myself in" in the presence of Almighty God, notwithstanding the blurring music in the bus. This discipline of "shutting myself in" in the presence of God has really served me well, and I have maintained it to date. The Holy Spirit always comes through and gives me a Rhema word either for me, somebody else, or the church.

---

**Remember**

*You must learn to "shut yourself away" from the world and "shut yourself in" in the presence of God if you want to hear His voice.*

When Habakkuk waited expectantly in God's presence concerning the existing situation in Israel, the Lord spoke to him and directed him to write down the revelation (Hab. 2:1–2). The Lord, through His Spirit, still speaks to those who tabernacle in His presence waiting to hear what the Lord has to stay. Sensitivity to the voice of the Holy Spirit is critical to being led by the Holy Spirit.

> **Remember**
>
> *Sensitivity to the voice of the Holy Spirit is critical to being led by the Holy Spirit.*

## Learn to Listen to the Inner Witness

God's ordained route for communicating with us is from His Spirit to the human spirit (Prov. 20:27). The human spirit communicates with the soul, and the body carries out the message the soul communicates. The fall of humankind corrupted this God-ordained route of communication as we lost the ability to receive God's Spirit. However, as part of our salvation, God has restored His original means of communication with us.

If you are born again, God communicates with your regenerated human spirit through the Holy Spirit. The voice of your human spirit is called the *inner witness* in scripture. The Lord guides us through our inner witness. Though inaudible, the inner witness speaks to us just as a traffic signal lights with green, amber, and red lights tell drivers and pedestrians when to "go," when to "stop," and when to "get ready to stop" or "go with caution." The "green light" of the inner witness signifies "you're good to go ahead." When the Spirit's "green light" is flashing, you will sense a serene inner peace. On the other hand, when the "red light" of the inner witness flashes, you lose your peace about an action or decision you've taken or are about to take. The "red light" indicates "no, don't go" or "you did wrong."

A couple of months ago, while in the company of a close friend,

I thought of sharing a joke, but the Holy Spirit started flashing the "red light" to indicate "don't do it." I quipped, "Isn't laughter good for the heart?" The "red light" kept blinking more intensely, but I ignored the warning and told the joke. To my surprise, the person totally misunderstood the joke and became extremely offended. Just then, I understood why my inner witness was flashing the "red light." I lost my peace instantly and apologized, but my friend refused to accept my apology, making my situation worse.

## Maintain a Pure Heart

We must rid ourselves of any and every known sin and filth and renew our minds by the washing of the Word of God (Heb. 12:1; Romans 12:2). Remember God's Spirit residing in you is holy and can only use vessels that are set apart for His exclusive use. Our bodies are the temple (dwelling place) of the Holy Spirit, and we must, therefore, honor God with and in our bodies and spirits (1 Cor. 6:19–20). When we do, the Holy Spirit will impart His divine characteristics to us.

## Follow the Leading of the Spirit

The test of sonship to God is to be led by the Holy Spirit: "For all who are led by the Spirit of God are sons of God" (Rom. 8:14 NIV). The word *sons* in this passage signifies mature children. Therefore, this verse of scripture implies that Christians who allow the Holy Spirit to lead them grow to become mature children of God.

The more you allow the Holy Spirit to lead you, the more you mature spiritually. It can also be inferred that we must play an active role if we want the Holy Spirit to lead us into spiritual maturity. There are several ways by which the Holy Spirit leads. He may lead you through your own regenerated human spirit (inner witness), the written Word of God, your sanctified conscience (inner voice), visions, or prophecy.

If you fill your spirit (heart) with God's Word and your mind is cleansed and renewed, you will be in harmony with the Holy Spirit. In that situation, you can be sure that your desires are aligned with those of God and the Holy Spirit is leading your life. You must follow His lead one step at a time. You must yield to His promptings and flow with Him. Remember you can only *expect* the Holy Spirit to lead you if you *let* Him.

## Chapter 12

### Yield! Yield! Yield!

*There is no limit to what God can do through
a person who is yielded to the Holy Spirit!*

Dave, Mike, and I had just finished putting up the last set of banners and posters for our upcoming Gospel event, which was scheduled to take place the following week. Exhausted from long hours of trekking up and down the city, I slumped into the open arms of my bed, which sat invitingly at the left corner of the room. I had barely lain on the bed for five minutes when I fell into a trance. In the trance, I saw myself lying on my bed when suddenly I heard a gentle knock on my window. It was Rosemary, one of the two sisters who were supposed to host the guest speaker, Brother Bheki.

"Brother Bheki is here!" Rosemary told me in the trance.

"What?" I exclaimed.

"He said he realized he had misread the date when he arrived at the airport and had come to bid us goodbye and return to the US," Rosemary explained.

"No way," I said.

Just then, I heard a gentle knock on my window. Not sure

whether I was still in the trance or back in reality, I jumped out of my bed—and there stood Rosemary.

"Brother Bheki is here," she said.

Confused and not quite sure which realm I was in, I told Rosemary about the trance.

She gently but firmly assured me that Brother Bheki had arrived from the United States for real—one week before the start of the program.

To cut to the chase, I went with Rosemary to her house and saw a tall, handsome young man with the most wonderful smile.

He gave me a bear hug as if we knew each other and said, "Well, Brother Emmanuel, I just came to say goodbye to you folks. I'm sorry, but I can't stay for another week. It's all my fault, and I apologize."

I told him about the trance and assured him that God would use the "mistake" to glorify Himself.

In those days, we did not have cell phones, and very few homes had house phones. I quickly trekked the one and half miles distance to our ministry president's house and informed him about the new development. An emergency leadership meeting was called, and we unanimously decided to hold the program that very week—beginning the next day—in order to accommodate Brother Bheki's travel schedule. Wow! Talk about mountain-moving faith!

It was a big step of faith. Would people come? How would people know about the sudden change in date? In addition to not having mobile phones, there was no internet or local radio station to announce the change in date. We quickly went out and changed the dates on as many of the posters and banners as we could and trusted God to do the rest.

When Brother Bheki saw our faith and eagerness to receive his ministry, he marveled and was moved to stay for the impromptu program.

That evening, Rosemary, Sabina (Rosemary's elder sister), and their mother hosted Brother Bheki and me for dinner.

*The Holy Spirit*

After dinner, Brother Bheki asked, "Do you see the angels of God around this table?"

Of course, we couldn't see any angels.

"Well, the angels of God are here, and they are ministering comfort and love to you guys," he said with a smile. "Did someone pass on recently?"

We informed him that the father of the two sisters had died a few months earlier (the widow was sitting opposite Brother Bheki). Brother Bheki assured us that God had sent His angels to comfort the family and assure them that their father was in the bosom of the Lord. The sisters' dad had given his life to the Lord at one of our programs a couple of years before his death. We knew he had died in the Lord, but Brother Bheki's vision provided additional comfort and assurance that God cared about the pain of the bereaved family.

In my correspondence with Brother Bheki, he described himself as a teacher and a prophet, and we saw him operate very beautifully in his God-ordained offices. Whether he was ministering from the pulpit or interacting with us informally, Brother Bheki literally lived in total submission to the Holy Spirit and stood ready at any time to speak for the Lord. During the five days Brother Bheki spent with us, he always ministered with power, simplicity, and clarity. When He taught the Word, he made it come alive. He taught the most profound truths in a way that even a child could grasp.

Another thing that really amazed me was the way he interspersed his teaching with prophetic utterances, word of knowledge, and word of wisdom. For example, in the middle of his teaching, he would pause and smile as if some unseen person had just whispered something to him. He would say, "Well, the brother at the corner there, here's what the Lord is saying," "The sister over there in red blouse, the Lord just told me to inform you that," or whatever the Lord had given him. After that, he would go right back to where he left off in his teaching. It was beautiful!

Being with Brother Bheki was like living in the presence of the Holy Spirit 24/7. During the first two days, he never gave me a "word from the Lord," though I spent most of my time with him. When I asked why, he smiled and said, "Because the Lord hasn't given me a word for you."

On the third day, while I was playing table tennis with him, out of nowhere, Brother Bheki said, "Well, Brother Emmanuel, here's what the Lord is saying: 'Your faithfulness shall be greatly rewarded.'" He went on to speak into my future ministry, and every single word he uttered has been fulfilled.

More than anybody else, the Lord used Brother Bheki to demonstrate to me that there is no limit to what God can do through a person who is yielded to the Holy Spirit. He was the very embodiment of a life that is completely yielded to the Holy Spirit. He literally lived in unbroken fellowship with the Holy Spirit. It didn't matter what we were involved in—Brother Bheki was in tune with the Holy Spirit and was always ready to speak for Him.

I met Brother Bheki when I was a few months shy of twenty one years old—and he was twenty-five—and I never ceased to be amazed about how such a young man could have such depth of knowledge, wisdom, and understanding. More importantly, he selflessly yielded to the Holy Spirit and boldly proclaimed God's Word.

**The Yielded Lifestyle**

My brief interaction with Brother Bheki taught me that we don't need to struggle to hear God's voice, know His will, or live a victorious life. I learned from Brother Bheki's lifestyle and ministry that successful Christian living requires a mix of two important factors. First, we must develop a reverential relationship with the Lord Jesus through constant obedience to His revealed will and pray in the Spirit consistently. Second, we must remain connected to the Lord by voluntarily yielding to the leading of the Holy Spirit. The more we walk by the written Word and follow the leading of the Holy Spirit, the more we will live above the natural realm. Brother Bheki's life taught me that it is possible for us, as God's children, to live in the Lord's presence constantly and consistently. There are three great keys to doing this. The first key is yield, the second key is yield, and the third key is yield.

The Holy Spirit is looking for *yielded* vessels to use. He does not coerce. He only uses those who voluntarily place their lives in His hands. The Holy Spirit is seeking yielded people through whom He will demonstrate His power, character fruits, and grace to this dying world.

Yielded people understand that they are not in charge of their lives—the Lord is. They understand that they don't call the shots anymore—Jesus does. They have relinquished control of their lives completely to the Holy Spirit. They have voluntarily submitted control of their minds, tongues, emotions, will, and every part of their being to the Holy Spirit. Yielding to the Holy Spirit is a continuous process. It is a lifestyle. It is a personal decision. In other words, the yielded lifestyle must be intentional and ongoing.

The yielded lifestyle is sacrificial, but it is a price worth paying in the light of the prize:

> And so, dear brothers and sisters, I plead with you to give your bodies to God because of all he has done for you. Let them be a living and holy sacrifice—the kind he will find acceptable. This is truly the way to worship him. (Romans 12:1 NLT)

Since the body is the house of the soul and spirit, presenting our bodies means presenting all of ourselves to God. God demands complete yieldedness! He demands nothing short of total surrender to Him. In view of all that God has done for us, total surrender is the least act of worship we can offer to God.

When we totally surrender to the Holy Spirit through prayer and obedience to God's Word, the Holy Spirit imparts to us the mind of Christ. We won't struggle to hear God's voice. Instead, the Holy Spirit will reveal the mind of God to us when we yield to Him and stay yielded. We will simply flow with Him. We will be transformed into the image of Christ, we will become more and more like Christ, and His glory will engulf us (2 Cor. 3:18). These are some of the blessings we can expect when we yield to the Holy Spirit. I don't know about you, but I believe the yielded lifestyle is worth its salt.

I am persuaded that God never intended the Christian life to be struggle. God's intent is for us to live in the power of the Holy Spirit. The grace by which we were saved is the same grace that sustains us throughout our walk with God. In other words, since we were saved by grace through faith, God expects us to continue to live under grace by faith. Having begun the race by grace, God does not expect us to live the Christian life in our own effort or by keeping a set of rules. The same measureless grace that saved us is available to carry us through the Christian journey.

The gateway to God's grace is submission to the Holy Spirit. The key to enjoying a struggle-free Christian life is yieldedness to the Holy Spirit. The yielded lifestyle is what I call living above the natural plain. It's a lifestyle where God's supernatural realm becomes natural to you.

**The Example of Paul**

Saul, who later became known as Paul, is a good example of a man who was completely yielded to the Lord. As a matter of fact, Saul learned the lesson of yielding to God the hard way. Having received the highest education in the best educational institutions of his time, Paul was obviously a proud young man. Utilizing his direct access to the corridors of power, Saul volunteered to pursue and crush the early church, thinking he was championing the cause of Judaism.

For a little over a year, Paul seemed unstoppable as he and his team of zealots terrorized the church—hounding believers into prison and getting others killed. The tide turned when Paul met the risen Christ on the road to Damascus. Here's the account as told by Paul himself:

> On the authority of the chief priests I put many of the Lord's people in prison, and when they were put to death, I cast my vote against them. Many a time I went from one synagogue to another to have them punished, and I tried to force them to blaspheme. I was so obsessed with persecuting them that I even hunted them down in foreign cities.
>
> On one of these journeys I was going to Damascus with the authority and commission of the chief priests. About noon, King Agrippa, as I was on the road, I saw a light from heaven, brighter than the sun, blazing around me and my companions. We all fell to the ground, and I heard a voice saying to me in Aramaic. "Saul, Saul, why do you persecute me? It is hard for you to kick against the goads." (Acts 26:10–14 NIV)

The majestic glory of the risen Christ, which was brighter than the midday sun, blinded Saul and knocked him to the ground. It does not matter who are when you encounter the Lord in His glory and power—you will have to yield. Now, totally blind and on his knees, Saul cried out in fear:

> *"Who are You, Lord?"* Then the Lord said, "I am Jesus, whom you are persecuting. It is hard for you to kick against the goads." So he, trembling and astonished, said, *"Lord, what do You want me to do?"* Then the Lord said to him, "Arise and go into the city, and you will be told what you must do." (Acts 9:5–6 KJV, emphasis mine)

This is a vivid picture of a yielded man: knocked to the ground, blinded, acknowledging the Lordship of Christ, and asking what he must do. Having thought that he could control his own life and destiny, Saul was astonished to learn that there was a superior power he had to submit to.

I am always impressed with the two questions Paul asked: Who are You, Lord? What do You want me to do, Lord? If we want to experience the Holy Spirit as our indispensable friend, we must seek to know the Lord more and more and ask Him to reveal to us His will for our lives so we can do it.

## Who Are You, Lord?

This is a very loaded question, especially coming from a young, proud man like Saul. Until now, Saul thought he was invincible and had it all. With the full backing of the Jewish leaders, he thought he was lord unto himself, only to discover a more powerful person knocking him down and blinding him with the brightness of His glory. For the first time in his life, Saul had to acknowledge Jesus as Lord. So, what can we learn from Saul's question?

If we want to experience the glory of God in our lives, we must allow Jesus to be Lord of our lives. As Lord, He calls the shots. We must allow Him to control our desires, decisions, and actions. If our desires are tangential to His, we must be willing to give up ours and go along with His will.

When Paul got to know Jesus and accepted the Lord's agenda for his life, he was content to pursue his God-ordained mission. The Lord used Paul to win thousands of souls to Christ, pioneer many churches, and raise a team of apostles, prophets, evangelist, pastors, and teachers. True to His Word, the Lord was with Paul, confirming his Word with extraordinary miracles and wonders.

It is important to point out that yielding to the Lord can also take us to unpleasant situations. Paul experienced persecutions, imprisonments, and many unimaginable kinds of sufferings. In the midst of them all, however, Paul's faith never wavered because he understood his calling.

## What Do You Want Me to Do, Lord?

This is definitely a question of total surrender to the Lordship of Christ. In just one encounter with the risen Christ, Saul abandoned his avowed agenda and surrendered completely to the Lord's agenda. Similarly, we must ask the Lord to show us what He wants us to do. We must throw away our own agendas and seek to fulfill His plans and purposes for our lives.

## Enemies of the Yielded Lifestyle

### I: Fear

Fear of the unknown is a major barrier to the yielded lifestyle. Fear diminishes God and elevates our problems. It is, therefore, the number one enemy of faith. Fear creates a distorted picture of God and His ability to care for us. It is a silent but powerful killer of faith. While faith says, "I am fully persuaded that despite my circumstances, God has the power to do what He has promised," fear essentially says, "I can't trust God with my life." This is why the Bible repeatedly warns us against letting fear have the better part of us and encourages us to exercise faith in God. God assures us of His constant, unfailing, protective presence.

> I will never leave thee, nor forsake thee. (Heb. 13:6 KJV)

> Fear not, for I am with you; be not dismayed, for I am your God; I will strengthen you, I will help you, I will uphold you with my righteous right hand. (Isa. 41:10 ESV)

> If God is for us, who can be against us? (Rom. 8:31 NIV)

Some people are naturally analytical and want to be assured of every outcome before they take a step. There's nothing wrong with being careful and thoughtful in our decision-making. I am like that. However, there's also a place for abandoning our own wisdom in order to trust in God's infinite wisdom. Those who trust in their own judgment find it difficult to commit themselves wholeheartedly to God and yield to the Holy Spirit. To them, yielding totally to the leading of the Holy Spirit is too high a risk to take.

Well, the Christian life is a risk. Jesus said, "If anyone would come after me, let him deny himself and take up his cross daily and follow me" (Luke 9:23 ESV). Denying yourself means saying no to your own plans and saying yes to Jesus. The cross signifies sacrifice and suffering, and following Jesus means being willing and determined to go wherever the Lord leads. Jesus demands total surrender of our own wishes, desires, and plans as a prerequisite for following Him. That's risky, but it's worth the risk.

In other words, being a follower of Jesus Christ is predicated on the assumption that we have already abandoned ourselves to the Lordship of Christ. It should, therefore, not be difficult for us to entrust our lives to the Holy Spirit and trust Him unreservedly to lead us throughout the changing scenes of life. Christianity is a lifestyle of faith in a loving, all-powerful God who wants us to trust Him with our lives and everything we have.

## II: Pride

Pride can be a good thing. It's definitely right to show pride in your child's performance in school, sports, or artwork. There's also the negative aspect of pride, and it is this negative pride that God warns us about: "Pride goes before destruction, a haughty spirit before a fall" (Prov. 16:18 NIV). Lucifer is a classic example. Having been created with extraordinary beauty, power, and skills, Lucifer became puffed up with pride and thought he could be equal with God. He mobilized one-third of the angelic host and sought to usurp God's authority. Lucifer's pride and haughty spirit led to his humiliation and downfall (Isa. 14:12–17; Ezek. 28:16–17).

This kind of pride has an exaggerated opinion of one's own importance, and it typically shows itself in arrogant behavior and conduct. Pride-filled people have an excessively high view of their own wisdom, abilities, and capacities. Feeling wise in their eyes, pride-filled people usually don't see a need to yield to the Holy Spirit. The pride-filled person's attitude says, "I can do without God; I don't really need Him." It's a dangerous place to be, especially as a child of God, because pride is the number one enemy of trust in God, which is a requirement for maintaining a harmonious relationship with God:

> Trust in the Lord with all your heart and lean not on your own understanding; in all your ways submit to him, and he will make your paths straight. Do not be wise in your own eyes; fear the Lord and shun evil. This will bring health to your body and nourishment to your bones. (Prov. 3:5–8 NIV)

There are many sources of pride. Pride typically emanate from our achievements, including our exceptional intellectual capabilities, extraordinary athletic or music skills, spiritual accomplishments, successful business careers, abundant wealth, and political achievements. Pride-filled people don't realize God gave them the acumen to accomplish the things they are so boastful of:

> For who makes you different from anyone else? What do you have that you did not receive? And if you did receive it, why do you boast as though you did not? (1 Cor. 4:7 NIV)

Pride may also manifest itself in terms of thinking of ourselves more highly than we ought to. The Bible admonishes us not to think of ourselves more highly than we ought but in humility esteem others better than ourselves (Ph. 2:3–5). Even in the exercise of spiritual gifts, we must constantly examine our hearts to ensure that we are not motivated by the desire to be seen or considered important. This is why the Bible instructs us to exercise restraint in our worship services and defer to one another (if need be) in the exercise of spiritual gifts:

> Two or three prophets should speak, and the others should weigh carefully what is said. And if a revelation comes to someone who is sitting down, the first speaker should stop. For you can all prophesy in turn so that everyone may be instructed and encouraged. The spirits of prophets are subject to the control of prophets. For God is not a God of disorder but of peace—as in all the congregations of the Lord's people. (1 Cor. 14:29–33 NIV)

Despite His high and lofty place position in the universe, God chooses to dwell with those who have humble spirits (Isa. 57:15). God delights in those who walk humbly with Him (Micah 6:8). If we really want to walk in harmony with God, we must humble ourselves and allow Him to be in charge (Amos 3:3). If we humble ourselves under the mighty hand of God, He will lift us up in due season (1 Pet. 5:6).

In our dealings with the Holy Spirit, it's important to remember that God's ways are usually different from our ways. Some of the ways the Holy Spirit operates may be contrary to our own thinking or what we are familiar with, but we must learn to yield to the wisdom, love, and grace of the Holy Spirit. Setting aside our own wisdom and pride to trust completely in the leading of the Holy Spirit is an integral aspect of our journey toward spiritual growth and maturity. I will illustrate with an example.

About a month ago, I was scheduled to lead our church's

prayer and miracle service. I prayerfully prepared five topics I believed God wanted us to pray about with the relevant supporting scriptures. When we got there, we began worshipping the Lord as we usually do. However, when I took over, the Holy Spirit began to signal to me that we should continue with the worship. We couldn't stop worshipping the Lord, and the Holy Spirit led us to spend the entire one and half hours in worship. It was beautiful. We just yielded to the Holy Spirit and flowed in worship. In the end, we were all filled with the Holy Spirit, our burdens were rolled away, and we were glad to have set aside our own plans and followed the leading of the Holy Spirit.

Humility is an indispensable quality if we really want to enjoy our walk with God. Humble believers understand that God's thoughts are not necessarily the same as our thoughts, and God's ways are not the same as our ways:

> As the heavens are higher than the earth, so are my ways higher than your ways and my thoughts than your thoughts. (Isa. 55:9 NIV)

The Lord's thoughts and ways—as revealed to us by His Spirit—may be different from our thoughts and our ways, but we must learn to humbly yield to His leading if we want God's best for our lives.

CPSIA information can be obtained
at www.ICGtesting.com
Printed in the USA
BVHW032010060819
555237BV00002B/2/P